The Power of Story

# THE **POWER** OF STORY

Connect With Purpose,
Unlock Your Influence

LISA GERBER

Published by Lisa Gerber

First published in 2024 in Sandpoint, Idaho, USA

Copyright © Lisa Gerber

www.bigleapcreative.com

Sandpoint, Idaho, USA

The moral rights of the author have been asserted.

All rights reserved. No part of this publication may be used or reproduced, stored in a retrieval system, or transmitted in any form or by any means without the publisher's prior written consent.

Every effort has been made to trace (and seek permission for the use of) the original source of material used within this book. Where the attempt has been unsuccessful, the publisher would be pleased to hear from the author to rectify any omission.

All inquiries should be made to the author.

Edited by Jenny Magee

Designed and typeset in Australia by BookPOD

ISBN: 979-8-9851385-2-8 (paperback)
ISBN: 979-8-9851385-3-5 (ebook)

# CONTENTS

| | | |
|---|---|---|
| Preface: | Mom's favorite blouse | 1 |
| **Part I:** | **The Power of Stories** | **5** |
| Chapter 1: | Stories are Magnetic | 7 |
| Chapter 2: | Storytelling is Influence | 15 |
| Chapter 3: | What Story is Not | 29 |
| Chapter 4: | The Ethics of Storytelling | 33 |
| Chapter 5: | The Fear of Making it About You | 37 |
| Chapter 6: | When It's Not Your Story | 41 |
| **Part II:** | **The Storytelling Habit** | **43** |
| Chapter 7: | The Journey to Get to Know You | 45 |
| Chapter 8: | Be a Changemaker | 49 |
| **Part III:** | **The Three Qualities of Powerful Stories** | **59** |
| Chapter 9: | Make It Real | 63 |
| Chapter 10: | Make It Relatable | 95 |
| Chapter 11: | Make It Riveting | 119 |
| **Part IV:** | **The Collective Impact** | **143** |
| Chapter 12: | Influence is Everything | 145 |
| Chapter 13: | Build a Story Library | 149 |

| Chapter 14: | The Lasting Power of Story | 155 |
| Chapter 15: | What's Next? | 161 |

| Who is Lisa? | 163 |
| References | 165 |

# PREFACE

# MOM'S FAVORITE BLOUSE

When I was 16, I participated in a summer abroad program in France. As I packed for my trip, I begged my mom to borrow her favorite silk blouse for the Bastille Day celebration. She reluctantly gave in to my pleas of "What could possibly go wrong?".

On the morning of Bastille Day, I was excited to lay the blouse on the ironing board. As the hot iron touched the material, I heard a hissing sound. I'd burned a huge hole in mom's best blouse.

What had gone wrong? I had an adapter, not a converter. An adapter changes the shape of the plug so you can plug your appliance into foreign outlets, but it provides a false sense of security, tricking you into believing that you have a good connection. On the other hand, a converter not only adapts the plug, it changes the voltage to match your device.

I ruined my mother's favorite blouse because I came in too hot with the iron. I was in a foreign land, and I didn't match the energy to the outlet.

Stories are energy, and storytelling is an energy exchange. If we come in too hot, we risk blowing fuses and losing attention. If we come in with too little energy, we fail to even turn on the lights.

I work with brilliant and passionate people who know their stuff and do everything they can to make the world a better place. Yet, despite their passion and depth of knowledge, they lose their audience because they come in too hot and blow fuses with too much information.

You've met them—well-intentioned people who give too much information or data. You see them at the other end of the grocery aisle and quickly turn away, hoping they didn't see you. And when you meet them in the hall in the office, you pretend you're on the phone.

Other leaders keep their stories a secret. They think their story isn't interesting. They don't want to make it all about them. So, no story means no energy and no power. Keeping their story secret does no one any favors.

Does that sound like you? Are you hiding your light? Is your story a mystery? Do you struggle to tell stories that get others on board?

The trouble is that we can't afford to hide if we're leading a team, engaging with a community, raising funds, growing our careers or stepping into personal leadership.

> **It's time to stand in the power of story.**

It's time to stand in the power of story.

Anthropologist and storyteller Jane Goodall dedicated her lifetime of work to changing the way people treat animals and the environment. She said,

"If you can get to the heart with a story, you may not know it at the time, but people will go on thinking."[1] Our job is to get to the heart through story so people care about our ideas for change. What they do from there is up to them. The best we can do is get to the heart. Hopefully, they will go on thinking, talk about it, and do something about it.

The most influential leaders tell stories and the best stories have three qualities: They are real, relatable, and riveting. In this book, we'll explore these qualities and help you uncover the stories that make you real, relatable, and riveting. Each of us has it in us. We do not need to be someone we are not. We simply need to harness the power of story.

# PART I

# THE POWER OF STORIES

# 1

# STORIES ARE MAGNETIC

Why do stories draw us in? And what makes them more compelling than hard facts and data?

There is something special about a story that shifts energy. Think of your anticipation when the movie theater lights turn down and the screen lights up. Or when you're in a conference audience and the speaker starts into an intriguing story. We lean in, eager to know what's coming.

Humans communicate best through story.

Remember the last time you got together with a friend? Did you exchange facts and data? No, you shared stories. That's because our brain is wired for story.

When we hear a story, the hormone oxytocin is released into the bloodstream, which creates a sense of safety and trust. Often called the love drug, oxytocin is the same chemical released during a beautiful hug.

Our brains harmonize during a good story. Professor Uri Hasson and his team at Princeton University discovered that brain waves sync up between the storyteller and the listener. It's a phenomenon called neural coupling.[2]

But enough about the facts; let's use story to understand why we lean in.

I began a recent conference keynote with a story about my beloved Bernese Mountain Dog. It was relevant to my talk, not just a gratuitous story about Jackson, but I admit, it did feel like cheating. Who wouldn't be drawn to such a story? During the following Q&A, a woman confessed she had not been looking forward to the day, but "You had me at the start with the story of your dog". Our sad expectation of conferences is that we will be bored to death by PowerPoint slides and droning speeches.

Stories, however, help our brains process information. Even better, they deepen our understanding of a topic and help us connect to purpose and each other.

Leaning in comes from the anticipation of knowing we're about to get a hit of oxytocin.

There's a problem with facts and data. Cognitive linguist George Lakoff says people think in frames—what he calls unconscious structures.[3] In other words, we see, hear, and interpret things from our own experiences and perspectives. When we encounter facts and data, we run them through our existing structured beliefs, values, and experiences. If our mental frameworks don't support them, we dismiss the information but inevitably have some kind of emotional response or attachment.

That means facts and data matter less in changing people's minds. It's why Trump can say and do what he does, and his fans continue to support him. On the flip side of the political spectrum, it's also why the Dalai Lama can get away with things that many people would consider inappropriate.

Humans tend to make decisions emotionally rather than rationally. Facts and data inform, but stories transform.

The next time you want to make your clients, customers, or donors feel like you have hugged them, remember that telling a story produces the same effect without any inappropriateness or threat of a sexual harassment lawsuit.

## I'm your power converter

I help people to talk about their work in ways that get others to care.

I opened with the story of my mom's blouse to make it easy for you to connect with what I'm about. I am your power converter. I help you match the energy (your story) to the outlet (your audience).

Over the past 20 years, I've worked with leaders and teams in the private and nonprofit sectors to make change happen. I helped a municipality and Environmental Protective Agency garner public input by telling the story of a Brownfield cleanup project. I've led a storytelling effort for an education foundation that was credited with securing a difficult-to-pass permanent school levy. I've coached the leader of a conservation organization to secure a million-dollar grant. I've advised senior leadership of a global outdoor leadership organization through a multi-million dollar transformation to increase trust and employee satisfaction.

> Facts and data inform, but stories transform.

In this book, I'll share my experience and thinking to inspire you to new ways of communicating through the stories you tell.

While many storytelling books offer a stepped process to a great story, that's not my approach. You already know how to tell a story. You do it every day. It's innately human. I would not presume to teach you something you already do without thinking.

The real problem is different.

Either you are telling the wrong story, or you stopped working on your story too soon.

You don't have to be a master storyteller, nor do you have to have had something epic happen to you. You just have to match the right story with the right audience at the right time. When your stories are compelling, the telling part improves with time and practice.

## Bridging the communication gap

One morning, I walked into the kitchen, deep in thought about my impending skin treatment for pre-cancerous cells on my face.

My husband asked, "When are you going to start your stuff?"

Me: "I'm not sure. I'm trying to find a period of time where I don't have to show my face publicly. Maybe after my speaking engagement in Los Angeles."

Him: "I meant your coffee. So we can go on the dog walk."

We take our morning walks with our coffees. I thought he was referring to my skin treatment because that was on my mind. He was thinking about the dog walk. As George Lakoff reminds us, we hear and see through our own experiences.

That moment of disconnect was minor and easily remedied. Imagine how much greater the potential for misunderstanding on a topic more significant than the morning dog walk.

What's on my mind isn't necessarily what's on your mind.

Likewise, just because I have an idea for change doesn't mean that you have the same idea. We must meet our audiences where they are. The power of story lies in matching the energy to the receiver. Remember my mom's blouse?

Many of us struggle to talk about our work in ways that get others to care. It's hard to admit this because we've dedicated our lives to our work, but our strength becomes our barrier. Our deep knowledge, the very thing we are distracted by, causes us to lose sight of what our audience knows and needs.

Our history shapes the way we hear, understand, and respond to stories. The childhood stories we were told shape our worldview. We hear the news through those perceptions of the world. Our role is to tell stories that appeal to the fundamental good in people, to their desire for a better world. That's what influential leaders like Jane Goodall and climate scientist Katherine Hayhoe do when they tell stories that bridge misunderstandings and disagreements.

I believe that when people find and share their stories with the world, everything gets better. Imagine what your story can do for you and your community.

That's the power of story and the point of this book.

# This book is your ally

This book isn't about telling stories. It's about the influence that comes with telling stories. Stories are the currency of conversations, which build relationships. When we touch people's hearts with stories, they think and then take action.

I've worked in hospitality, in corporate settings, with nonprofits, entrepreneurs, and thought leaders. We are all leaders. We're leading projects, companies, and households. So when I say leader, I mean every one of us. Taking it further, I've observed and thought deeply about what turns an influential leader into a change-making leader.

> What's on my mind isn't necessarily what's on your mind.

We tell stories through different lenses, from highly personal to broadly organizational, and bigger, more complex ideas that fit the global landscape.

Part One explores why stories are so powerful. We can be more strategic when we understand what underpins a story.

In Part Two, we'll look at how people get to know you, what the conversation needs of you, and how to develop a storytelling habit.

In Part Three, I will unpack the three qualities of powerful stories: real, relatable, and riveting, and explain how leaders can embody them in everyday communications. This section is designed as a list of Frequently Asked Questions, so you can hop around depending on what you need right now. Each question is accompanied by a story type and prompts for you to tell that story. Each of the three qualities, Real, Relatable, and Riveting, opens with a story to show how we use it to connect individually, then through our organizations or work, to solve social issues and understand global perspectives.

My goal is to help you expand your library of stories so you can make connections that match the context of your conversations. I'm less interested in *how* you tell a story and more interested in *what* story you are telling.

Let's begin.

# 2

# STORYTELLING IS INFLUENCE

## The currency of conversation

Amy had butterflies in her stomach as she took the microphone during a client event with major vendors and sponsors in attendance. The purpose of the evening (and of her message) was to thank people for attending and to acknowledge sponsors and vendors for their contributions. She also needed to raise money. It would be a tough ask to interrupt the animated conversations in the room, so Amy knew she needed a compelling message.

She told a story.

Amy described how she was rejected from the high school cheerleading squad, not once but twice. She said she was excited that the event theme was a tailgate party because she could finally dress as the cheerleader she always wanted to be. Everyone laughed. She had their captive attention and went on to share her message.

Later, several people approached Amy to share their own high school rejection stories. Others sought her out to have a good laugh.

Your stories don't need to be epic dramas or of life and death—Amy's certainly wasn't. Stories start a conversation and give the listener something to latch onto, respond to, and pull on to discover more. Stories aren't about what happened; they are about connection. That's what people crave.

It turns out this connection thing is as essential to human existence as food and shelter. In his book *Social,* Matthew Lieberman says that while connection is fundamental to daily life, leaders are often more focused on getting things done than connecting.[4] Fewer than 5% of the 60,000 leaders Lieberman interviewed were good at achieving results *and* creating connection. Results and connection aren't mutually exclusive. We need both. Imagine if relationship-building was a class, like productivity or economics or business management 101.

Often considered a soft skill, storytelling is essential for any modern leader. Those who want to make ideas happen have to get others on board. We can't operate in isolation. We need relationships built on trust and understanding.

The power of story is the energy exchange and connection that happens when two or more people interact and feel valued, seen, and heard. There's no judgment. Each person feels stronger and nourished after engaging. Story is the primary vehicle for this; it's how we communicate best. Think of any of your most important relationships—with your significant other or your best collaborators. We are storytellers at our core.

Yet, we don't make time for quality connections. Perhaps surprisingly, most teams are not truly connected in this time of hybrid and remote work, and abundant connectivity tools.

Connectivity does not equate to connection. We are so busy getting things done that messages are abbreviated into acronyms and jargon. There's no room for story and plenty of room for misunderstanding.

It's time to step back and get engaged. Global management company McKinsey undertook research in 2021 to find out why employees were leaving in The Great Resignation.[5] Their key findings? While employers reported the primary reason was to get more money, employees said they were leaving because their managers didn't take the time to see, listen, or understand them. They felt disengaged and wanted more. On its own, that misunderstanding is a pretty big disconnect.

> **Connectivity does not equate to connection.**

So. how do we fix this level of human disengagement? Through conversations that connect, where individuals feel seen, heard, and understood, and where there is an exchange of vulnerability and trust.

It's not that managers have bad intentions. It's because they weren't taught Relationships 101. They learned what it took to do their work and advanced in their careers because they achieved results. However, they didn't understand that connecting was fundamental to engagement between managers and employees. And they certainly didn't learn that exchanging stories is the basis for that connection.

## What do your employees need?

Given a choice, people prefer to work with leaders they relate to.

Who is the best boss you've ever had? What did you love about them? And how did that impact your work and your desire to show up each day? Now, think about your worst boss and the qualities they modeled. How did that affect your attitude and performance?

Employees stick around when they feel connected to their teams and understand how they fit in the big picture. They show up with purpose and passion. When they see behavior they don't understand, they make up stories that are rarely generous or kind. It's the perfect recipe for a toxic environment.

If your team is engaged, you are more likely to experience less turnover and deliver better customer experiences. Employees who feel seen and heard have greater job satisfaction and show up with purpose and energy. A 2022 Gallup poll found that teams that score in the top 20% in engagement realize a 41% reduction in absenteeism and 59% less turnover. Yet, 65% of employees do not feel engaged in their work.[6]

When the people in your organization show up with passion and purpose, that tells the best story about your organization. There is an undeniable cultural shift when team members deliver outstanding experiences to customers and clients.

## What do your clients need?

Trust is vital. In a study by BoardEx, 88% of professional service respondents acknowledged that relationship management is critical to their practices, and 94% of investors refer their financial advisors when they trust them.[7] Despite this, financial advisors say their biggest challenge is emotional engagement. They get portfolio management, but emotional management? Not so much. Money might be numbers to financial services professionals, but it's emotion to investors.

Billy Lanter is a fiduciary investment advisor at Unified Trust Company in Lexington, Kentucky.[8] He says, "The pressure is on for advisors to show their value outside of traditional portfolio management. The superior experience clients are willing to pay for is a personal relationship with an advisor who not only understands their goals, but is managing their portfolio in accordance with those goals."

## What do donors need?

Philanthropists are continually rethinking their giving strategies, and relationships drive those decisions. A 2021 study by NPOInfo found that 61% of donors give based on how efficient nonprofits are with their money (trust), 42% give in response to a personal story of someone or something you helped, and 44% give based on the organization's connection to purpose.[9]

Your employees, customers, clients, and donors are just like everyone else in your life. They crave connection and connection to purpose. Something bigger, something grander.

In his foreword to *Ecological Literacy: Educating Our Children for a Sustainable World,* David W. Orr wrote, "The planet does not need more successful people. But it does desperately need more peacemakers, healers, restorers, storytellers, and lovers of every kind. It needs people who live well in their places. It needs people of moral courage willing to join the fight to make the world habitable and humane and these qualities have little to do with success as we have defined it."[10]

When we lead with story, relationships follow and everything gets better. So, how do you do it?

## Give people handholds

You can create a perfectly manicured experience and shield your audience from rough edges, polishing every surface to a slick sheen. Your website can have beautiful stock images that make you look impressive. Your bio may read so professionally that anyone would want to work with you, yet you leave out the parts about your gap year in Europe or time out for parenting because they make you look inconsistent. Because, you think, why would anyone care?

Your organization's story is a timeline of all your organizational milestones, but where are the people? Is it because you think your team is too small and you want to appear larger than you are? Or perhaps you have a large team and we get to see a grid of professional headshots on white backgrounds instead of people doing what they love.

You can let people see the real you through loose threads or tiny handholds that give them something to explore. Allow them to know you, see you, and relate to you. In doing so, they will get to know themselves a little better.

"Be who you are, not who you think you should be." That's the advice of author and researcher Brené Brown.[11] The posh you could be anyone, anywhere. The real you provides a far richer experience—one that people will remember and talk about for decades.

When you get real, you become memorable. You develop relationships that make work and life more meaningful, productive, and fulfilling.

> When you get real, you become memorable.

The story of the real you doesn't only impact your audience. It has a real and intangible effect on you, the teller. It can change the trajectory of your career, as it did for Taylor Swift.

## Shake it off

Whether or not you are a fan of her music, there is no arguing that Taylor Swift is one of the most influential storytellers of our time, meaningfully connecting with millions of people around the globe. During her 2023-24 Eras Tour, she sold out stadiums of 70-96,000 seats multiple nights in a row in major cities across the globe.

The Netflix documentary *Miss Americana* shows two turning points in Swift's career.[12] The first was when she decided to be more politically outspoken despite her team's advice. The second was when she stopped letting criticism of her dating life and her popularity affect her and boldly shared her experience of that critique and love. She embraced her stories of heartbreak and the imperfections in her voice. The stories in the songs came deeply from the band's heart and collective experience. They won their first Grammies for this album.

It's another example of how everything can change when we shake off others' opinions and step into who we are. When we avoid the polished, staid and manicured experience, we get to stand out instead of fit in.

The impact stories have on your audience is crucial. While difficult to quantify, a story's impact on the teller is palpable. Notice it next time you open up about yourself with someone, and you'll understand. We tend to show up more comfortably when we feel accepted for who we are.

## We are the problem

Humans are inherently storytellers, yet we seem to lose the art of conversation when we enter the professional setting. We speak in timelines, facts, and data. We use graphs and PowerPoint decks laden with bullet points, industry jargon, and ridiculous buzzwords. We don't take the time to get to know each other because we don't have to be friends with the people we work with and we all have so much stuff to get done.

I know the art of conversation is lost because I hear a different version of it every day.

The leader of a nonprofit organization calls me because they are doing amazing work, but no one knows about it. They feel invisible and ineffective. How can they be continually overlooked when another organization doing similar work (albeit unethically, they might add) is on fire?

A CEO wants senior leaders to better engage their teams and the community they operate in. These leaders are doing the work, but there are many misperceptions and objections around the work they do. They are not doing a good job of telling their story, debunking the myths or managing their reputation.

A financial advisor gets in touch because she needs to be better at relationships so she can retain and grow her practice. She was disappointed in a recent potential client meeting as she thought she came off as vanilla. "I didn't feel on my game." Financial advisors are everywhere and investors have so many choices. How can she stand out in a sea of the same? Why isn't she getting referrals? How can she tip the scales from hustling for work to attracting inbound requests?

Relationships and connections fix invisibility, misunderstanding, and stagnant revenue but are often considered a low priority because there are always more pressing work responsibilities, family obligations, and household duties.

The deadlines, reports, performance reviews, emails, and meeting schedules are urgent, so they get your attention. Relationships with your team and stakeholders are important but less urgent so they don't. Stephen R. Covey's work on productivity centered around how to shift your focus from the urgent, reactive things to the seemingly less pressing but far more significant projects.

Most of us don't have the luxury of ignoring our relationships. Change (and good leadership) doesn't happen in a vacuum. We need people.

## Everything is at stake

What if you don't take the advice in this book?

I was part of a communications team during a multi-million dollar organizational transformation. Change requires effective communication because people handle change differently. Our team collaborated. We disagreed respectfully. We worked through problems and found solutions. We produced awesome work, but it wasn't noticeable until that work ended abruptly and communication took a lower priority when a new senior leadership team stepped in.

At that point, employees wondered why they were hearing about things like no compensation increases next year through an all-employee forum and not from their direct bosses. "That didn't feel good," they said—at a public event. The new senior leadership team were surprised. They took communications for granted and had let the comms team go as an unnecessary expense. If you are silent, culture withers and dies.

In a meeting with a department manager, I asked about her connection to senior leadership. Without hesitating, she said, "When I haven't heard from them in a while, I assume they are fighting a lawsuit." I reported this finding to the CEO, who was dumbfounded by the impact of their lack of communication.

Stories matter. If you are silent, people will create their own stories.

You have a choice. Either you can take control of the narrative or someone else will.

You likely have no idea of the opportunities you miss by not connecting through story. The stakes can be enormous and you might not even know. It brings to mind what happened in the virtual conferencing space in the years before the COVID-19 pandemic.

In 2017, I received an email from the software company LogMeIn with the subject line:

*Important information about your account.*

I ignored the email a few times because I thought I didn't have an account with LogMeIn. It wasn't until the third email that I realized I did; I use LastPass, a LogMeIn subsidiary.

The email was to inform me of a merger with Citrix. Here's what it said:

*To our valued user,* (Actually, they do have my first name, as I'm a paid subscriber. So, not only could they have taken the time to segment their audiences based on what product we pay for and eliminated my confusion over being a customer of LogMeIn, they also could have taken a few moments to do a mail merge and address the email to me directly. These details tell your community a story without telling a story. Ironically, their opening line made me feel the very opposite of valued. Anyway, back to the letter.)

> *To our valued user,*
>
> *We're happy to announce that on January 31, 2017, LogMeIn, Inc and Citrix Systems, Inc's GetGo subsidiary (A wholly owned subsidiary consisting of the GoTo family of products) completed our merger. For users, the new LogMeIn will offer best-in-class capabilities across a much larger combined portfolio—immediately increasing choice and value—while featuring the scale, resources, and world-class talent required to accelerate innovation and address future needs.*[13]

I don't even know where to begin with how awful this message is. What does it even mean? How exactly will the merger do any of those things they promise? Why will it do those things? This was a perfect opportunity to connect with various audiences and they missed it. They could have given specifics and outlined scenarios as examples. Tell people a good story about how you will make their lives better for being a "valued user".

As the final kicker, the email ended with:

> *Please note that replies to this email are not monitored– please do not reply to this email. As always, please feel free to contact us here: <provided a URL link>*

They have someone monitoring form submissions on the website, but can't give them access to monitor replies to an email they sent telling us how awesomely world-class they will be now that they can scale, innovate, and meet future needs. Really?

Don't just pretend to care. Actually care.

Why not include a letter from the two CEOs with a vision for the future? Or how two CEOs will be better than one? Draw an analogy to something we can all relate to. Provide some context. Explain what the merger means to the paying customers. And if it doesn't mean anything, why not tell us so?

> **Don't just pretend to care. Actually care.**

The people you want to reach and influence know when you are simply checking an item off your to-do list. (Tuesday: email paid subscribers regarding the merger.) Instead, honor every communication as an opportunity to tell a story and create meaningful relationships.

I work every day with brands struggling to build audiences and make connections, so I hate seeing opportunities like this squandered.

So, what can we learn from the LogMeIn example?

About a year after I received that email, the Boston Business Journal reported LogMeIn lost $1.4 billion in market valuation. In short, the CEO said they were seeing a drop in contract renewals because they created too much friction and didn't deliver on promises. I would argue that clients left because the company failed to tell a compelling enough story for them to stay.

In an ironic twist, John Greathouse, from GotoMyPC claims the merger between LogMeIn and Citrix would never have happened if he had told a more compelling story to his own partners decades ago.[14]

Greathouse wanted to pursue remote access products like online meeting platforms in the early 2000s. His partners and investors weren't convinced they should move forward, and Greathouse attributes that to his lack of the right story. A small company called 3am Labs did get their investors on board and soon became LogMeIn, rendering GoToMyPC almost irrelevant.

As we all know, virtual meetings soon become critical to everyday life. Zoom came out of nowhere to beat everyone in the space with its ease and simplicity. It makes you wonder how things might have turned out differently for GoToMyPC had they told a better story.[15]

You can't know what opportunities are wasted when you fail to tell the right story. But the ripple effect is apparent if we treat every interaction and moment as a chance to make a connection.

This idea of withholding your story is a relic of another time. The world now calls for relationships. Relationships are built on conversations and story is the currency of conversation.

When we lead with story, everything gets better. When we fail to do so, everyone loses.

# 3

# WHAT STORY IS NOT

Words matter, so it's important to be clear on what we're talking about. What do we even mean by story? It can be an account of incidents or events. A description of real or imaginary people told for entertainment. A plot or storyline. A piece of gossip or a rumor. Even a false statement or explanation—a lie.

While there are many ways to define a story, the purpose of this book is to help you talk about your work in a way that gets others to care. I know; my book, my rules. So, here's my definition of story through that lens.

First, a story is not a chronology or timeline of events. This is the greatest mistake organizations make. For evidence, click on the *Our Story* page of most websites. A string of dates is history, not story.

> **A string of dates is history, not story.**

Story is a vehicle for communication. Back and forth, we share experiences and ideas. We all have many stories to tell that are part of a bigger story—the story of us.

A story can be an image. I'm reminded of the tragic story of the dead Syrian boy, washed up on the beach in Greece. No one paid attention to the Syrian refugee situation until that photo was circulated.

A story can be a sentence. Google six-word stories, and you'll find plenty, such as the one often attributed to Ernest Hemingway. "For Sale: Baby Shoes. Never Worn."

Stories come in different shapes and sizes. It's a narrative of people or events with a plot, told in conversational language. This description doesn't always have to be true, but it's helpful as a baseline as we spend the next 100 or so pages on the topic.

## Stories are told, heard, and inferred

George Lakoff and other linguists acknowledge that you can tell a story, but you can't control how it's heard. We interpret stories through our own experiences and perspectives. We'll go deeper into this in Part Two of the book when we discuss frames of reference and relatability.

## Actions speak louder than marketing

Although this book focuses on the narrative of words and pictures, your listener's experience of you and your actions are also, intentionally or unwittingly, part of your story. Everything you do is part of your story from the uniforms your people wear, the customer experience you provide, and the order confirmation emails you send. It even extends to how you let customers break up with you.

After 15 years with my online bookkeeping provider, it was time to make a change. I went into the software to cancel my subscription and found the option after much poking around. But I couldn't do it online as cancellations had to be done by phone. That phone call took 45 minutes. They were sorely misled if they thought making it difficult to leave would make me stay. Instead, I have a negative story about a 15-year relationship that was fine until the very end. Naturally, I tell that story and not all the other good stuff. Bad experiences reap bad stories, which reap bad dividends.

Your stories may influence their action, but your actions also influence their stories. We call this theorizing. Humans take a bunch of events and link them to make meaning.

If you sign up for a ladies' mountain bike clinic and they overlook details like sending a link to the gear list, the meeting time and place, and other important information, it's frustrating. It makes you wonder what other details they have overlooked and whether they will keep you safe in the clinic.

When you get the experience right, people can cancel their subscriptions easily, phone calls are answered by a human and an employee thinks to include a link to more information. If a picture is worth a thousand words, an action is worth a thousand stories.

Good strategy influences right action, which influences a good story.

A good story creates understanding and conveys emotion. It's a human-to-human interaction. If you wouldn't say it aloud in a social setting, then it's likely not a story.

Stories are moments of transformation or revelation.

A family doesn't have access to fresh water. A single mom finds herself in a gas station, having filled up her tank with only $7 in her pocket. Two strangers exchange a gaze from across a crowded room. A six-year-old comes out of her shell to play her fiddle in a recital.

> Stories are moments of transformation or revelation.

Every story has a setup and a resolution, with some kind of lesson or takeaway and something to do or be differently. But the moment makes the story.

If we lead with story it must have a purpose and good intention.

# 4

# THE ETHICS OF STORYTELLING

## Give them a reason

A moral imperative provides a reason for your audience to take the right action. It is a universally agreed principle that compels them to act, for example, breaking into a burning house to save a child. Every story you tell should have a moral imperative.

Chad Littlefield, co-founder of We and Me, shared a story demonstrating how important it is to engage your audience and value their time.[16] Former Facebook COO Sheryl Sandberg walked into a meeting and identified exactly how much the meeting was costing the organization based on the salaries of the individuals sitting there. Then she said, "Let's get straight to it".

This story is a powerful reminder to never take our audience's time and attention for granted. If we are telling a story, it should have a purpose and be of interest to them. There must be something in it for them, and getting there shouldn't take longer than necessary. Every word in that story should serve a purpose. We'll get deeper into this soon.

# Should you really tell that story?

This chapter will help you avoid a common pitfall in storytelling: Is my story inappropriate or over the top? You don't want to seem manipulative or exploit a situation. How much is too much?

Strategic storytelling is not a soft skill; it's essential—one where we tell stories to make change happen. Change is the keyword here. We aren't telling stories just for fun; there's a fine line between influence and manipulation. Good intentions will keep you on the right side of that fine line.

Your stories should have a purpose. I find it helpful to have a purpose statement that answers the question, "Why am I telling this story?" Maybe it's to show the importance of customer service. Perhaps you need to illustrate how the state budget works. Your purpose might be personal, to remove barriers so others will trust and open up to you. Your team needs to understand how important this project is to the bigger picture.

A strong purpose keeps you focused strategically, clarifying your message and bringing it to life. It sets you up to be compelling.

It's a good idea to pressure-test your statement with a follow-up question: "What's in it for them?"

You may want to get personal and reveal something about yourself, but is that boasting? Is it drawing attention? Do they actually care? What will they get out of this story? Why should they care?

No one cares about your anniversary or your new website. (Do you care about theirs? They are just being polite.) However, if you fully funded your endowment on your anniversary so that 100% of donations go directly to doing good, you'll have a story that others will care about.

If your new website features a diagnostic that will help someone get from A to Z, you have a story. The story might be about you, but it must be in service to them. If you aren't being of service, you are being indulgent.

> **If you aren't being of service, you are being indulgent.**

Whether it's an email campaign or one-to-one conversation, a keynote speech to thousands or a business pitch to a small group, you are engaging in a conversation that is part of a bigger story – the story and the experience of you. Like a gift inside a gift, your audience uncovers new treasures, getting to know and understand you along the way.

## Check your intention

Be clear about your intention. Purpose is what you want to accomplish, while intention is where you are coming from. Is your story from a place of generosity? Or is it transactional? In other words, are you giving freely or asking for something in return?

Generosity is a beautiful intention. Your story is intended to educate, inform, create deeper understanding around a situation, create relatability, or underscore an idea. The bottom line? Every story should be in service to your audience.

Selling, patronizing, and bragging are self-indulgent. You're telling the story to garner attention, for kudos or congratulations. Perhaps even to get sympathy. Such stories come with dubious intentions.

Story is not a tool to get people to think something that isn't true. That's manipulation—an imbalance of power with one person seeking to influence others in a harmful way. Ethical storytelling is a generative energy. It's an exchange of power in a gift.

# 5

# THE FEAR OF MAKING IT ABOUT YOU

Are you thinking you don't want to make it about you? Perhaps the situation in question isn't about you, and getting personal would be inappropriate. Maybe. But if you are impacted, your people want to know.

## It's never really about you

Remember Amy's story about rejection and the people who approached her afterward to share their rejection stories? Once told, a story belongs to the receiver. Even though the story is personal to you and your work, effective storytelling is significantly about the listener. The story serves the listener, who is better off for having heard it.

You might fear sharing your story, knowing that others will make of it what they will. But here's a better thought: share the story knowing others will find something of themselves in it and be better for that. Something will change for them: a feeling, a thought, a behavior, or an action.

When you hold your story back, everyone loses.

# Don't be the hero

You may be the protagonist of your story, but don't be the hero. The hero saves the day. The protagonist goes through some stuff. The best stories show us as imperfect leaders.

Kintsugi is the Japanese art of pottery repair. Shards of broken pottery are mended with gold, making the repaired piece more beautiful than the original. It's the ideal metaphor for highlighting our imperfections for others to know and see.

If you stay off the pedestal, you should be safe. Stories fall flat when you pat yourself on the back. It is downright cringeworthy when someone tells a story and then explains why it makes them so wonderful and important.

For example, after you've told the story about how you run a business, take your kids to their soccer games, and run all over the place like a madwoman, don't say, "I'm a Type A woman". (Cringe!) Humble bragging, editorializing, call it what you want; your audience will see through you. You can be factual and descriptive without telling them what to think. Let others draw their conclusions.

At the start of the novel *Daisy Jones & The Six*, author Taylor Jenkins Reid paints a picture of Daisy Jones.[17] Daisy says: "I had pretty bad insomnia for a long time, even when I was a kid. I'd be up at eleven o'clock, saying I wasn't tired and my parents would always tell me to 'just go to sleep'. So in the middle of the night I was always looking for quiet things to do. My mom had these romance novels hanging around so I would read those. It would be two in the morning and my parents would be having a party downstairs and I'd be sitting on my bed with the light on, reading *Doctor Zhivago* or *Peyton Place*. And then it just became a habit. I would read anything that was around. I wasn't picky...I found a box of history biographies on the side of the road one day...I tore through those in no time."

What does this tell you about Daisy? That she was a good kid given the circumstances she was raised in. Her parents ignored her, and instead of getting into trouble, she read and took control of her life. Instead of being the hero, she is simply describing what life was like.

If you're worried about whether you're making yourself the center of the story, consider these questions. What's your discomfort in sharing the story in question? Are you the wrong person to be delivering this message? Why? Are you in a room with really smart people? Acknowledge it. What is wrong with what you have to say? What is wrong with the environment?

These questions are designed to give you the confidence to share your story—or decide that it's not appropriate. If it feels icky to talk about yourself, it might be that the story doesn't pass the Ick factor test.

What's the real reason you're sharing the story? It should be in service, not indulgent. Examples of indulgence include looking for sympathy or accolades. Flip the narrative and the language so your audience can instead:

- learn from a process or a hardship along the way
- understand the inner workings of a system and why it has to be the way it is. Connect it to a policy.
- underscore a powerful idea with a personal account.

You won't feel uncomfortable talking about yourself if you are in service to your audience, not perched on a proverbial pedestal.

# 6

# WHEN IT'S NOT YOUR STORY

Sometimes, we tell someone else's story, not just our own. It may be a client, someone you've helped (a success story), or a story you heard that perfectly fits your purpose and intention.

Let's talk for a moment about privacy, attribution, and permission.

## Protect privacy

I've worked with numerous nonprofits helping people in domestic abuse situations or other private matters where storytelling is vital yet delicate. There are a couple of ways to handle this. We can make the person anonymous by changing their name or doing what NPR does and giving them a code name, like Patient A1A. Sometimes, that isn't enough—especially if you are in a small community and the details are enough to identify the real person. In that situation, a composite story works well, merging multiple stories or changing details such as gender, title, role, and geographic area to protect the person's privacy further. I do this several times in this book.

Whatever we do, we disclose how we have changed the story. For example, we might say that the person's name or certain details have been changed to protect their privacy.

If the story didn't come directly from you and your lived experience, always acknowledge its source. This is basic courtesy and gives credibility. You don't want to pass off a story as yours, then have it uncovered and be accused of appropriation. Attribution is the high road; take it always.

> **Attribution is the high road; take it always.**

You'll need permission to share a client or patient story. (Amy gave me permission to share the cheerleading story about rejection.) People are usually happy to give it if the story will help others. If they express any concern, be clear on why you want to use their particular story. It's not to exploit their plight; it's to…do what? To help others who find themselves in a similar situation?

Your industry will likely have regulations you must comply with, so I won't go into those here. If you aren't familiar with those guidelines, make sure you are before telling a story that isn't yours to tell.

# PART II

# THE STORYTELLING HABIT

# 7

# THE JOURNEY TO GET TO KNOW YOU

While first impressions are instant, relationships develop over time. Understanding how people get to know you is worthwhile because the conversation needs something different at each stage of the relationship. You don't have a single story; you have many. Knowing which story to tell starts with understanding the journey to get to know you. You wouldn't tell the same story at a job interview, on a first date or in a parent-teacher meeting.

Where are you on the journey to helping people get to know you? And what do they need from you before they'll take action?

## Invisible: Batman

Batman works—anonymously through the night, saving the day. He is the invisible hero. Invisible leaders are often highly productive in isolation, believing it is faster to do things themselves than to explain them to others. Getting on with things is certainly faster than connecting through a story. We all need to be expedient at times, getting into action and making things happen.

The problem is that significant change doesn't happen without a team. Introverts don't have the luxury of working alone. As much as I like to preach that what other people think about us shouldn't matter, what others think does matter. Both sides of the coin hold true. It's about reputation.

You will be overlooked, irrelevant, and unnoticed if you don't tell your story. You won't get things done because not enough of the right people know about you.

What the conversation needs: If you are invisible, your stories need to generate attention. That often means having a quick headline or scroll-stopping moment ready so that when people walk by your proverbial table, they see your hand reaching out and stop to learn more.

## The technical nerd: Dr. Spock

Star Trek's Dr. Spock is deeply knowledgeable and passionate. He's a subject matter expert, but people don't really understand what he says.

The technical nerd's deep expertise is an advantage until they have to talk about it. They know so much and tend to flood people with that knowledge. They're like a stuck record. Everyone avoids them.

Facts and data are important, but they don't influence change. They might lend credibility to your case, but only if people take the time to make sense of it.

When did you last sit, feet up, gripped with excitement, and open a book of industry jargon, facts and data? If you are using the usual arguments and appeals, you aren't cutting through the noise.

What the conversation needs: If you're a technical nerd, then you'll do best by telling stories that generate interest. Most of your stories should focus on educating your audience about a problem or a gap you solve. People are meaning-making machines, and stories are an opportunity to bring statistics to life and make meaning of data with an example or metaphor. We'll talk about those in Chapter 9. Your audience won't take the time to decipher your data unless you make it easy for them.

## The misunderstood leader: Otto

Otto Anderson is a 63-year-old curmudgeon, played by Tom Hanks in the film *A Man Called Otto*. Cynical and grumpy, all Otto's neighbors fear him. What they don't know is that he lost his wife six months earlier and is grieving her deeply. He puts up a front to protect himself. However, one neighbor sees something in Otto and goes on a mission to help him. When they get to know the real Otto, the neighborhood dynamic changes for the better, and Otto becomes happier, too.

Sometimes we act as someone we are not—or as someone we think we should be.

Being misunderstood can lead to many challenges.

The misunderstood leader often ends up in this situation because they've kept secrets. They are like vaults, a characteristic that is valuable in close friendships but not in leadership.

What the conversation needs: When we are misunderstood, our stories must work hard to earn trust and shift perceptions. We do this through our reputations and by addressing the tough topics.

## Intriguing: Seinfeld's Kramer

Charismatic and popular, *Seinfeld*'s Kramer character knows everyone and always has a fun fact or piece of trivia to contribute to the conversation. He's charming in many ways, but his entertainment value is far higher than his motivation or inspiration value.

We are intrigued and pay attention to these people. They have many interesting stories that capture our attention, and we think, "Wow, I had no idea!"

When you are intriguing, people follow you on social channels, read your emails and attend your presentations. You are memorable, which is great, but they stop short of taking action.

What the conversation needs: Being memorable and interesting is nice, but we really want people to do something. When you spur your audience with great stories, you drive them to action. They show up, volunteer, sign petitions, and knock on doors for you. Your stories have built trust, so people are willing to give time, which is one of their most precious assets.

# 8

# BE A CHANGEMAKER

In the remarkable TV series, Ted Lasso is brought to the UK to coach a British soccer team, a sport he knows nothing about. He doesn't pretend to be someone he isn't. While he doesn't know much about the technical details of the game, he understands how to motivate the team and bring them together. His speeches and actions galvanize the team, lead them to win games—and provide great comedic fodder for delightful TV watching.

When you combine all the elements of a great storyteller, you become a change-maker and a powerful force for good.

Matt Church is my mentor and one of Australia's top leadership speakers. He says there is a certain charisma in someone who stands so clearly in their power.

I'm sure you've experienced this, whether it's performing an activity you love, in a particular phase of your life or a fleeting moment.

Change-makers are powerful because they attract the right people. They garner attention when they speak and people are ready to drop everything to do what they suggest. Steve Jobs described it well when he said, "The most powerful person in the world is the storyteller."[18]

Let's start a movement!

## Don't limit your impact

In September 2023, Taylor Swift encouraged her social media followers to register to vote. She wrote, "I've been so lucky to see so many of you guys at my US shows recently. I've heard you raise your voices and know how powerful they are. Make sure you're ready to use them in our elections this year!"

That day, 35,000 new voters registered, a 23% jump over the previous year and double the number of 18-year-olds.[19]

Societal change doesn't happen in a vacuum; people make it happen when they connect with people. Leaders who wish to remain relevant in today's relationship economy must connect through meaningful stories. Influencing change doesn't happen without individual and collective relationships.

The iconic change-makers I reference throughout this book have consistently demonstrated the three qualities of powerful storytelling. They are real, relatable, and riveting. There's more on this in Part III.

These leaders have developed a storytelling habit that builds influence and elevates them beyond the transactional or the rational to the emotional. In the absence of emotion, we make decisions rationally, such as purchasing a box of paper clips, where the decision typically rests on price. You aren't selling paper clips.

When done well, stories take your audience by the hand and carry them along with you. You attract employees who deliver incredible experiences to your stakeholders and customers. They decide to come along with you regardless of price or any other factor because they are so emotionally invested. The relationship is what matters. That explains why people will pay more for a pair of Patagonia running shorts when they could get a similar product for less elsewhere. They are emotionally attached to the brand and what it stands for.

Relationships are why people will fly from around the country to attend your event, as they did for Amy and her cheerleading story. It isn't a rational decision; it's emotional. They do it because they love the beautiful connections and memories Amy and her team create each year. They feel included and don't want to miss out.

The opposite of rational is not irrational—it's emotional. Emotional connection is at the heart of influence and impact. Decisions that might not make sense on paper happen because you swept them up in your storytelling and created a relationship that transcends the transactional.

Your job is to use story to get to people's hearts. That's how you help them to know and care about your work.

## Curiosity gets you noticed

Reflect on the journey to get to know you. Some haven't heard of you yet; you are like Batman, the hero in the background, but invisible. Others are aware but not interested; you are like Dr. Spock and your communication style is technical. Some don't get what you do or have heard mixed messages about your work; you are misunderstood like Otto. Meanwhile, others are intrigued but haven't committed to you; like Kramer, you are intriguing but don't inspire much activity.

In your personal life, the stories you share with your spouse at the end of the day will differ from the story you share with someone sitting next to you on an airplane or with a close friend on a walk in the woods. Likewise, in business, the story you tell changes depending on where someone is on the journey to know you.

You are complex (as is your organization), so you will have many stories to tell. One story can never give the full picture. After all, could you tell one story about yourself and expect people to know you?

As Jane Goodall suggests, we must meet people where they are to connect to their hearts. To inspire action, tell the right story. In Part III, you'll learn about the many types of stories you can tell to bring people on the journey to know you.

Before we start telling stories, we need to understand what the conversation needs from us. Telling is just one half of the conversation; listening is the other. So we should start by listening.

A change-maker is attentive and curious. To get to the heart with story, we have to know what we're working with. The best way to know is through curiosity and listening skills. The late Stephen R. Covey had it right when he wrote that "most people do not listen with the intent to understand; they listen with the intent to reply."[20]

Here's an example of the best kind of listening. At Sydney Airport, a man and his young son were paying for their snacks ahead of me. After taking his change, the young boy thanked the cashier. His father leaned over and whispered in the boy's ear, "When you thank someone, give them eye contact to show respect". That moment was a great reminder of the power of attention. It also confirmed my faith in humanity.

The power of story is rooted in the power of attention and the intent to listen to understand. It's not just about telling stories. It's about evoking and listening to other stories.

Fundamentally, people want to feel seen and heard, yet we talk so much about storytelling and very little about story listening.

I start every storytelling workshop with a brief exercise where people pair up and share a story about themselves. Invariably, they are surprised to learn something new and fascinating about people they've worked alongside for years. This activity never fails to shift the energy in the room and bring people together.

How well do you know your colleagues and partners? How about your customers and clients? How much time or effort do you spend on getting to know them?

In my 20s, I worked at the Four Seasons Hotel in Seattle, serving breakfast in the Georgian Room. We started work at 5 am and had a great deal of prep to do before service began at 6 am. One morning, the guy assigned as busboy for my station didn't show up for work. I was angry and resentful because it left me with a lot of extra work early in the morning.

At the end of the shift, our manager gathered us to tell us that the team member had died in a car accident on the way to work. I was horrified at my behavior and saddened at his loss. His name was Tenzin, and he was from Tibet. Later, I learned that his four-year-old son is recognized as the reincarnation of a Buddhist monk, and he traveled to Tibet a year after his father's death to be enthroned as a lama.

I didn't know anything about Tenzin. He was just someone I worked with, and I never showed any interest in his life or his family. I simply saw him as a person who made my work easier. Had I asked a few questions, I would have learned the story of his son first-hand rather than reading it in the *New York Times*.[21] Tenzin would have made my work more meaningful, not just easier. Consider that story from a leadership perspective. Does your team know each other?

Curiosity makes team engagement better.

Curiosity helps us connect to the communities we serve. How will we know what story to tell if we don't know who we're talking to? Where are they on the journey to know us? What questions do they sit with? What are their doubts? If they are a customer or client, how was their experience with you? What do they say about you when you're not in the room?

The answers to these questions help you as the storyteller understand what the conversation needs of you so you can begin to make that connection and match the story to the need. As we explore the three pillars of storytelling in the next section, the story prompts at the end of each chapter will help you do this even further.

When we listen well, we make better, stronger, and more lasting connections.

To be good at questioning, we have to park our assumptions. Curiosity (and the lack of it) is led by what we believe we know— our innate assumptions. As we are largely unaware of these assumptions, breaking their hold is very difficult. We don't know what we can't see.

Frogs see light and dark so clearly that they can spot a fly in the air and capture it with their tongue. They see what they need for survival. Yet they don't see much more than that, so they don't know what else is out there. The same holds true for humans. We see what we need to, but we have no idea there is so much more. If we can release our assumptions and open our minds, as Stephen Covey said, when we listen to understand rather than to reply, an entire world opens up.

Try it as an experiment in your next social setting. Instead of responding to your friend's anecdote with your own experience, ask them to say more. Ask exploratory questions and stay in story-listening mode. Resist the urge to tell your own story.

Doing so requires two things of you: presence and attention.

## Cultivate a habit

When you cultivate a habit of genuine curiosity, watch what happens when it expands into your work setting. If you need more proof before you put this into practice, consider your closest friends and colleagues—those you respect the most. What qualities do you admire most about them? I bet they are great at listening; it's a very attractive quality.

Being attentive is also about being present. Picture yourself involved in a conversation yet distracted by other people in the room. What are they saying? Who's having a more interesting conversation? Meanwhile, you seem to be paying attention in your conversation, but you are not. At the next pause, you nod or intervene with your own experience. That is what I call boomerang attention. It's asking someone what they are doing tomorrow, only to wait for an opportunity to tell them what you are planning.

Good attention requires presence, focus, and genuine interest. *New York Times* columnist and author David Brooks says there is no dimmer switch on attention; it's either on or off.[22]

Curiosity invites us to ask open-ended questions that delve into a topic. Say a client sends you an email thanking you for the experience. You might ask them to tell you more about it. What exactly about the experience helped them? What was the impact? How did it change them for the better?

Attention and curiosity go hand in hand in helping you discover great stories.

## Attention in

Stories are everywhere. They are in your everyday experiences and told to you by your customers, clients, and stakeholders. You just need to pay attention and ask questions.

Attention can be focused internally or externally. That's attention in or attention out. Attention in means reflecting on what has happened to you today and in the past. These musings fuel stories about you.

We'll explore in detail what it's like to get personal, but for now, I want to set the scene for you to recognize what would make a great story.

I was on a trail run in the wilderness with a group of friends who were much faster than me. I found myself alone, scrambling up a mountain of loose rock, crying, "Why do I do this to myself?" "Why can't I be happy staying home watching TV?" Those thoughts turned into a story about balancing happiness and ambition, as I recognized that I wouldn't be happy just watching TV. I'm too restless and goal-driven.

Stories are everywhere when we focus our attention inward and reflect on what is happening around us. Change-makers watch for themes that relate to conversations they have or need to have and take note of them for later use.

How do you watch for and find stories in your daily life?

Look at what happened. Stories are more than an account of events but it's a start.

Now, find the relevance for your audience. What was the event about? What did you learn from it? What might others learn, or how can they benefit? Can you use this as an example to explain a concept? Can you show instead of telling something? Does the story bring something to life?

Be curious about a transformation, how someone felt before and after a moment. These make for interesting stories.

## Attention out

Attention out means you know where people stand regarding your messages and objectives. You pay attention to what they say, whether you are in or out of the room. You know what questions are on their minds, where they might object, and what they hold deeply to be true.

Investors in an aid organization working to combat malaria in Africa might have failed without attention out. In *A More Beautiful Question,* Warren Berger tells the story of Acumen, a nonprofit that funds purpose-driven initiatives such as an aid organization bringing bug nets to Africa.[23] Their solution to combatting malaria was mosquito nets. When they listened to the people using the nets, they learned the nets looked nice and helped them sleep better. They didn't care as much about the health benefits. Knowing this, Acumen and the manufacturer changed how they talked about the nets.

Berger quotes Jacqueline Novogratz, founder and CEO of Acumen, as saying, "You just don't know about people and what drives them until you listen to them until you spend time sitting on the floor, listening to someone tell you their story." If the aid organization hadn't been paying attention and asking good questions, they would have missed important information.

Stories are everywhere, every day. To get to the heart with story, we have to know what we're working with. What does our audience need from us? Or what does this conversation need of me right now? Developing a habit of attention and curiosity will help you notice stories more regularly. The story types and prompts sections in following chapters will help you do that.

# PART III

# THE THREE QUALITIES OF POWERFUL STORIES

## The connection conundrum

I always believe that story makes everything better, but there's a risk, right? Story requires us to be vulnerable because we are getting personal. If we are rejected, we take it personally. That is why Taylor Swift's team advised her against being more outspoken about her ideas. They wanted to protect her from being disliked. If she plays it safe, they think, everyone will like her. The same goes for regular people like us. If we play it safe, everyone will like us.

It's a conundrum—a connection conundrum. In our desire to be universally liked, we lose the ability to be uniquely loved.

There's a conscious decision involved here. It will take courage to put your story out in the world. Inevitably, someone will reject it and, at its worst, someone may even troll your story. That doesn't stop the world's most influential leaders (and pop stars). We can see how their stories make an impact, from conservation and education to climate change and female empowerment. These leaders focus on the people who love them, not the ones who troll them. I invite you to join today's icons who are changing the world for the better—one story at a time.

> In our desire to be universally liked, we lose the ability to be uniquely loved.

There are three qualities to powerful stories. We'll cover these in depth in the coming chapters.

First, powerful stories are real. They ground your messages in evidence. To be real is to be genuine, not imitation or artificial.

Real leaders use real language. They don't get overly technical or speak in jargon. They show instead of tell. They talk about what they know is on people's minds without beating around the bush or couching their language in platitudes.

The second quality of powerful stories is that they are relatable.

People act on what they understand. When you balance the energy to the power source, you are relatable. You blow the sockets if you come in too hot with your message. Come in too low, and you lack any power to ignite anything.

Relatable leaders are not afraid to be vulnerable. They show they care, and they stand for something that matters. They know how to meet people where they are in the conversation, and they make distant ideas understandable.

And finally, powerful stories are riveting. They elevate the energy and the conversation. They are engrossing and compelling because the world of possibility is irresistible. The power of story is not power over another but a generative power that elevates everyone.

Riveting leaders show people what is possible. They show up true to themselves. They frame stories with a growth mindset and connect to purpose.

## The other side of the conundrum

When your stories are real, relatable, and riveting, you attract an audience that is the right fit. They trust you, and you are all better for working together. It's about trust, relevance, and hope. All through story. I'll say it again. Everything gets better when we lead with story.

As we explore these qualities in the following sections, consider what stories you might tell that you haven't told before.

To be an effective storyteller, you have to tell the right story.

# 9

# MAKE IT REAL

## Ground your messages in evidence

Being real helps to make sense of facts and data. That bears repeating; facts and data inform while stories transform.

The power of story is grounding. Just as we ground wires to avoid electrical shock and fire, so too, leaders ground messages in reality and evidence because stories allow us to show rather than tell. When we are real, we develop trust and give people confidence that they are in good hands.

> **Facts and data inform while stories transform.**

For example, say you want someone to believe you are trustworthy. My dad had a favorite line our family has joked about forever: "Trust me". What kind of response do you think that evoked? If you want people to trust you, you can't just ask for it or tell them they can. That kind of statement plants the opposite idea in their head. If dad prefaces a situation with "Trust me," I know there is a reason for me *not* to do so. My Bernese Mountain Dog knows this. If I call him back when he's walking ahead, he inevitably looks ahead before doing what I've asked, assuming there must be something I'm steering him away from.

Instead of *asking* for trust, you have to *earn* it through your actions. Your stories serve as proof.

If you want people to think you are great at customer service, will explaining that you are customer-focused, results-driven, and client-centered convince them? Think again. That's meaningless jargon. If customer service is an important part of your story, offer real stories of delivering on your words. These are the stories that help you shift perceptions. Story makes real whatever you want to tell them.

Being real is showing up as yourself, not someone else. It means no more jargon or buzzwords. It's about being transparent and open.

Real leaders:

- show instead of tell
- communicate complex messages simply
- address difficult topics.

Let's look further at how to use story to build credibility, clarity, and transparency.

## What have you done?

### Story type: Your bio

The story of you establishes credibility because it gives you the power to show instead of tell. Yet, in many ways, I feel personal stories are the hardest to write. I bumped into this when, as a guest on a podcast, I was asked: "Tell us about your journey to becoming a strategic storyteller?"

You'll appreciate that with me being a storyteller, the pressure was on big time to tell a good story. I've done it many times in speeches and new business discussions, but this was a podcast and the story needed to be different based on the context. I needed to find the thread that connected to the audience and the podcast theme. It had to be grounded in what I'd done to lay the foundation for our conversation.

Your bio should answer the question that is on every listener's mind: "Why should I listen to what this person has to say?" The version of your personal story you deliver will change because you have many facets.

It's better to be prepared, so take an inventory of everything you've done and create different stories for different audiences. My work in nonprofits gets called on in some situations, and my corporate work in others. My background in hospitality is often a helpful foundation. And somehow, I weave a story of skiing being central to my existence and how it's brought me full circle. (That's what makes me relatable, so we'll get to that.)

You'll have a short intro for meetings, events, and proposals, and a longer story for your about or bio page.

## Story prompts

Take an inventory of what you've done and accomplished in your life and career.

What impact have you had? Think beyond outputs and go to outcomes.

Identify a recurring theme or feeling. Maybe a word keeps popping up for you.

Perhaps there was a moment when everything changed. This can be the central focus of your story.

Enough about you. What about your company or the work you do?

# What do you do?

## Story type: The micro story

The journey to get to know you is varied, so you'll want a stable of stories that get to the heart in different circumstances. Sometimes, you need a one-liner describing who you are and what you do. Sometimes, the one-liner is about your company. I call it the micro story. It's the quickest way to get attention, spark interest, stop the scroll or the walk-by, and give them a reason to want to know more. Remember Hemingway's six-word story: "For Sale: Baby Shoes. Never Worn." It says enough to be a story yet leaves us wanting more.

Your micro story is typically found on the home page of your website and is a quick introduction for someone new to you and your organization. Given just a few seconds to stop someone in their tracks (or their scroll), what would you say?

Many companies like to talk about being the leading provider in a sector. Others talk about their longevity. "Doing such and such for 100 years." "World-class" is another favorite. But these terms are meaningless and don't tell a story.

When you tell me you are world-class, not only do I not know what that means, but I wouldn't believe you if I did. I doubt you've ever read that ACME company is a leading provider of world-class solutions and thought, "Wow! Take my money!"

No one cares. And we want people to care. We have to be real to get people to care.

Bill Gamber founded Big Agnes, makers of sleeping pad systems for camping trips so you "never slip off your pad again". He could have said, "world-class leading provider of sleeping pads", but that's not a story. The story is that good sleeping pads are hard to find because we slip off most of them. That's relatable and real.[24]

A good story is rooted in a problem that you solve.

Typically, people have a problem in mind, and they may have no idea of what the solution might be. Your job is to speak to the problem instead of immediately presenting a solution. And you can do so with the best intentions, even though the solution is what you are selling. We'll explore this more in Relatable.

Your micro story could address the problem and the solution that adds value to the person with that problem.

Here are a couple of thoughts if you're wondering how to solve multiple problems for many different groups.

There are levels of abstraction from concrete detail at the bottom to the bigger picture at the top. Can you level up the abstraction and find an umbrella statement that encompasses all the problems you solve?

You have many micro stories, and the story you choose to tell depends on who you're talking to. At a conference, on the airplane, at your kid's soccer game, a donor meeting, a board meeting, an investor pitch, different landing pages on your website. The micro story changes, even though the truth does not. Many things can be true at once.

Your micro story is a great start. Play with it. Give them enough to want more.

### Story prompts

Fill in the blanks in this script then play with it to make sense for you.

I/we help [these kind of people] who [have this conflict or problem] to [your solution] so they can [feel or do something].

# What's the company story?

## Story type: About Us

At some point in the journey to get to know you, someone may want to know more about the company. Take a moment to think about when that might happen. Would it be after they've met you or someone at an event? Or when they've come across you on social media. Did they see your micro story and want to know more? What do they need at this point?

They want to know you are real people and that they can trust you. (Among other things.)

People who connect to you and your story are more likely to work with you. Your "About Us" company story can be humanized and interesting. Websites full of stock images and AI-written text won't cut it. AI might be able to get you started, but don't let it do all the work!

The human need for connection is real and deep. People see through unreal elements with a sixth sense and find it repellent when we work too hard to attract them. Without the real human element, you will be overlooked and obsolete.

To transcend rational decisions, you'll need to get personal. That's a truth that even applies to boat sauce. Bobbie's Boat Sauce comes with a postcard of a boat anchored in a quiet cove. Scribbled in pencil on the front, it says, "Boat Sauce invented here". It even included the date and geographic coordinates. On the flip side, in handwriting, was the following story.

*Paul caught a fish off the side of the boat, and asked me what I was going to serve with it. Seemed like a good reason to clean out the fridge...and ended up being a brilliant idea! Tomato paste, pickle brine, garlic, ginger, fish sauce, etc. I just went with it! Served with grilled fish, jasmine rice, and the remaining cucumber. Tangy, a little spice...can't wait to try w/eggs. Maybe I'll sell it and call it "Boat Sauce!" Ha!*

*XOX, Bobbie*

Given the choice between a major corporate brand or a smaller brand like this, which would you choose? Personal doesn't have to be soul-baring; it's a handhold for people to feel part of an experience or a purpose.

If a boat sauce "About Us" story can be interesting, yours can be, too.

## Story prompts

Imagine you've just been assigned to write your company's story for the About Us page. You stare at the blank screen, wondering what to write.

You might start with the year you were established. That is a fine place to start, but you'll likely find yourself reciting the timeline of events. Many people confuse history with story. That's fine for your first draft, but let's make it better. Look at that data and ask yourself, "What is the story of us?"

Here are some questions and story prompts to consider.

(Your story does not need to answer all these questions; it's an attempt to draw out salient points that will inspire your story.)

Who started the company and why?

What was the moment like when the idea came into being?

What fundamental problem do you solve? Build out the headline. How did it become a problem? Who is affected by it? Why does it need to be fixed? What happens when the problem is fixed?

What happens when the problem goes away entirely?

What happens if people do nothing?

How do people feel when they have this problem? How will they feel when they are free of it?

Did the founders of the company experience this for themselves?

Find a moment of transformation and resist the urge to give a chronology. We want your story, not your history.

**We want your story, not your history.**

These are the stories that make you real. We've worked on establishing credibility with your audience through your personal story, the micro story (of you and your company) and your full company story.

This creates a solid foundation, but now we're ready to work on deep understanding through clarity. Story is a beautiful tool to make complex messages easy to understand.

## How do you communicate a complex message?

If you're thinking, "It's not that easy", this section is for you. Your message is complicated. You're in science, engineering, technology, or perhaps finance. I have some suggestions for communicating these ideas in more compelling ways.

We'll talk about the tools to simplify a message through story, how to focus your story for clarity and how to underscore an idea or word by expanding on it. Sometimes, you want to be brief, but sometimes, the moment calls for you to expand on something. We'll also talk about the power of choosing your language. And finally, clarity wouldn't be complete without addressing the misunderstandings about you and your work.

As a change-making leader, your job is to make the complex simple and understandable.

Humans are meaning-making machines, so we naturally try to make sense of your stuff. But most of us don't have time, so if your message is too hard to grasp, or long, rambling paragraphs of content, or loaded with data and technical jargon, we'll move on, leaving you feeling ignored and sad, wondering why no one cares about your thing.

Stories help time and attention-deficient audiences quickly understand you and your work. A story molds the ingredients into something easily digestible.

Your favorite news source does this for you every day. They curate events and activities from across the world, and bring you what they think you need and want to know. For example, you don't have time to read a full legislative bill, and even if you did, would you understand it? The news condenses it into a package or story you can easily consume.

As storytellers, our role is similar to a journalist. It's up to us to curate events and our work into a story that compels our audience to take action.

In other words, do the work for the people you want to reach. Make it easy for them.

Yes, I know, that's easier said than done. The main challenge is that you want to include the many layers in your story because you are proud or excited about it all. You think every detail, every fact, every piece of data matters. That's where hard decisions come into play. It's time to simplify the message. Your story cannot be all things to all people. There is no one-size-fits-all when it comes to storytelling.

## Story prompts

As always, be in service to your audience. Consider the key questions burning in their minds and prioritize your list accordingly. Remember that you are engaging in a conversation, even if you aren't physically with them, and it's not a literal conversation. Given the number of possible communication channels, how will you draw them in to learn more? Chunk down your story into simple singular messages. Trickle them out. Leave bread crumbs.

Have you ever stepped into a department store and felt so overwhelmed by the range of options that you walked out? Or have you flipped through a six-page restaurant menu that offers Italian, Mexican, and American cuisines? (I steer clear of those because they can't possibly do so many different types of food well, meaning they are probably mediocre at everything.)

That is what happens when you serve your audience a story with everything in it. They are bored or overwhelmed and run for the door.

## The Ponderay Front Yard project

Let me walk you through my process of helping the City of Ponderay, Idaho, tell a story about a complex waterfront cleanup effort so the public could get involved and understand what was accurate and what was misinformation.

I began by speaking to many experts involved to take an inventory of all the information. The cleanup had multiple moving parts involving different entities. There was an extension of a recreational trail, purchase of privately owned property, cleanup of toxic ground, and an underpass of a railroad so people wouldn't unsafely and illegally cross the tracks to get to the beach.

There were many benefits, including the connectivity of three communities, safer commuting, and better recreation. A big downside was that the cleanup of the toxic property would involve logging a forested area. Rumors circulated that the property would be developed into a luxury community and marina.

This is where smart people tend to get convoluted in their messaging. They want to tell the whole story right away. We had plenty of data like traffic numbers across the railroad tracks (people carrying kayaks and fishing poles), soil analyses, land pricing, community input, and renderings of the finished cleanup.

I took all this information and spread it out to catalog everything as if they were tools and implements on a tarp.

The questions I pondered included:

What is the end result or action we seek? How do we get to it?

What are residents of the community most worried about?

What is the one big problem we will solve with this project?

What happens if we do nothing?

After considering everything, it came down to one key idea: Access to the public waterfront is a precious asset for this community. With mountains in their backyard and the lake in their front yard, where do they want to go on a hot summer day? To the lake. They want to swim, walk, fish, kayak, throw sticks for their dogs, and skip rocks with their kids.

The problem was that the waterfront issue was complex, with a variety of owners, stakeholders, and challenges. But the public didn't care about that complexity, so we gave the story one name: The Front Yard Project.

We curated all the data and information and reduced it to a few words that helped lock the concept into people's minds. "Our front yard is a place to gather, and it's a mess right now. Let's clean it up and talk about how that looks."

> *Just because it happened doesn't mean it needs to be in the story.*

We didn't need to bog people down with irrelevant details like which organization was handling which bit. What mattered was that all the pieces blended to improve the front yard of this community. We met people where they were by taking a lot of potentially confusing material and finessing it into what mattered and what was memorable for time and attention-deficient audiences.

We did not withhold information. Once we captured attention with the idea that this project was about improving public access to the waterfront, anyone could read the longer version and dig into details with links and access to the data. It's important to note that we did not come in hot with a load of information. If you're interested, here's a link to a video that details the Ponderay Front Yard Project. https://www.youtube.com/watch?v=diMO6Y2eXck

Less is more. There's a story that recounts how Michelangelo was asked how he created his masterpiece, the statue of David. He said, "It was easy. I created a vision of David in my mind and simply carved away everything that was not David."

What if you approached each story like that? Create the vision in your head and the desired outcome or reaction. Then, instead of adding more information, strip away what doesn't serve.

You have it in you. Every person I work with has it in them. Toss everything out on the tarp and take a moment to assess. Get some outside perspective as you begin to shape it. Describe the story in your own words and see what happens.

Two approaches can help you simplify complex messages: one word and metaphor.

## Story type: One word

What is one single word that serves as a guiding light for your story? Are you serving it? Or have you wandered off course?

Salad Bowl is a great game for simplifying concepts into a single word. Each player has five pieces of paper on which they write the names of people: real or imagined, dead or alive, well-known or only known to the group. Combine the names in a salad bowl and divide into teams of three or four.

In round one, the first person on Team One draws a name and has one minute to get others to guess the name. The only rule is that you can't use first or last names. Once the time is up, the first person in Team Two does the same. It goes back and forth until all names are used. Teams count their points and return the names to the bowl.

Round two is the same concept, but they can only use three words to describe each person.

In round three, it's down to one word. That isn't as hard as it sounds because, by this stage, everyone knows which names are in the mix. You are essentially editing the longer story of each person into a single, unique word.

It's great fun to see which words are associated with different people. The last time I played, Ted Turner's word was "Montana", Billy Joel's was "piano", and Harry Potter was "children".

As I type this, I'm imagining you crafting your next story. A demon-type character on your shoulder is whispering, "But what about that other thing? Aren't you going to tell them about that, too?" (That character might even be real, like your boss or a board member!) It takes great discipline to swat that fiend off your shoulder. If you succumb to their suggestions, you risk overwhelming your audience. You push content at them rather than pull them in.

The habit of curating or editing your ideas down to a single word prevents you from cramming too much into your story. It provides clarity and discipline about your message.

## Story prompts

Next time you're working on a story or message, play a quick game of Salad Bowl. Start with round one and use all your words. Have at it. Then, go to round two, reducing to three words. Have the discipline to get to round three, then zoom back out and tell your message through the lens of the word.

## Story type: The metaphor

Are you a scientist, a financial advisor, or an engineer needing to explain a data-heavy concept?

Stories are beautiful when expressed as a metaphor, which is principally a way of conceiving one thing in terms of another, and its primary function is understanding.[25] Metaphor creates deeper understanding by bringing something outside of a person's scope of knowledge and showing it through something they do know.

*Braiding Sweetgrass* is one of my most beloved books.[26] Author Robin Wall Kimmerer is a professor of environmental and forest biology and a citizen of the Potawatomi Nation. She quotes the scientist and poet, Jeffrey Burton Russell, "As the sign of a deeper truth, metaphor was close to sacrament. Because the vastness and richness of reality cannot be expressed by the overt sense of a statement alone."

Kimmerer uses the metaphor of sweetgrass to set the stage for the book. "A braid of sweetgrass meant to heal our relationship with the world. This braid is woven from three strands…an intertwining of science, spirit, and story…".

### Soup for oil

Here's how climate storyteller Karishma Porwal explained the concept of OPEC to her followers on Instagram, using tomato soup as a metaphor for oil. She describes OPEC as the largest legal cartel on the planet.

"Imagine the entire world is obsessed with tomato soup. Why wouldn't they be? It's a classic. American companies that harvest American tomatoes do very well. Then, they start harvesting Middle East tomatoes to get richer and sell to the rest of the world. Then Middle Eastern countries decide this is unfair and band together to produce tomato soup, eliminating the US from the region. If everyone wants tomato soup, they realize they should horde it and release a small amount at a time so they can charge more and get very rich. Then brave countries stood up and said, 'We don't need your tomato soup. If we can't grow tomatoes, we'll grow broccoli and make broccoli soup or mushrooms and make mushroom soup.'" Karishma brings us back to oil, the dangers of fossil fuels and how they force countries to be dependent on cartels. Broccoli and mushroom soup are forms of renewable energy so countries can be independent.

Metaphor is a brilliant way to deepen our understanding of a complex idea and make it relatable. And, frankly, easier to pay attention to.

## Story prompts

Finding and using metaphors is challenging and will take practice.

Ask yourself what is this (message) like in their (your audience's) world?

Find an artifact, such as tomato soup or the power converter that I use to describe storytelling as an energy exchange. Explain that concept and then connect it back to your message.

### Story model: Words as speed bumps

I know this is contrary to what I've just said, but simplicity doesn't have to mean brevity.

We've talked about stripping away every word, phrase, and detail that doesn't serve the story. I'm usually a big fan of brevity. The satisfaction of replacing four or five words with one can be hard to beat. Some people like playing golf and hitting the ball just right, while others like leveling up in video games. Me? I just want to see how few words I can use to communicate something.

However, don't mistake simplicity for brevity. Every now and then, brevity needs to be sacrificed for clarity.

Yes, sometimes it takes more words to be clear, not fewer.

When given a choice, always choose clarity over brevity.

Here's an example. As I mentioned earlier, one of my favorite tricks when communicating something complex is simply to ask my client what they mean. They explain and we look at it all to assess the story. We pick the pieces we are excited about and assemble them into something clear, though not necessarily brief.

When we have complex messages to deliver, we can use our language to underscore ideas and reinforce understanding of a topic. As my client explained what their work involved, she used the word "proactive". I agreed that it was an apt description, yet it's such a big part of their work that I felt it deserved more than one word.

When people are in a hurry, they gloss over things. Maybe they don't take the time to think about what a word means. Or perhaps they have a slightly different interpretation.

So, instead, I suggested they say. "We solve problems before they become bigger and more expensive problems later." That is decidedly many more words, and usually I'd have huge satisfaction in simplifying, but sometimes more is, indeed, better.

We can use words as speed bumps. If you have a point you want to punctuate, and you want to be certain they get what you're saying, expand on that word and ensure the right perspective is captured.

Choose clarity over brevity; they are not mutually exclusive. Brief doesn't mean clear, and clear doesn't mean brief. As in all things storytelling, it's up to us to find the balance.

## Story prompts

Survey the facts and data on your tarp. Is there a moment of transformation you can center the story around?

What do you want them to think, feel, or do?

For that to happen, ask:

What do they need to know? Strip everything away that doesn't build up to or support the moment.

What change are we seeking?

Why does it matter to them?

## Story model: Real words only

Words are powerful, but they can also be weak and meaningless.

Being real through storytelling asks us to use *real* language. That means avoiding the weasel words of clichés and generic words and phrases that can (and will be) freely interpreted by the people you want to reach. "Amazing" and "world-class" immediately come to mind. What do they even mean? Think back to the email I received from LogMeIn, where they talked about "best-in-class capability". The entire email was riddled with buzzwords that meant nothing to me.

Technical language, or jargon, is another area where you can lose your audience. When we assume they know something that they really don't, our complex messages quickly lose their attention.

When an Environmental Protection Agency analyst rattled off a bunch of meaningless numbers and statistics with acronyms, I asked him to explain how above or below normal they were. I asked him to compare the information with evidence from a year ago. In the story, we provided the technical data in one sentence after explaining how toxic the soil was in terms the general public could understand. Make it easy for your audience to understand. They won't take time to decipher your complicated stuff, and you will wonder why you can't get attention.

It's the same for skiers. On ski days, they typically check the snow report for the resort they are visiting. We do this to decide what to wear, to be informed of conditions and unexpected closures, and to decide whether to go or stay home.

Some ski resorts treat the snow report like a marketing tactic rather than an opportunity to build trust and lasting relationships. Instead of describing the real situation, they sugarcoat it. For example, they won't use the word rain; they say "mixed precipitation" because rain is not good for skiing. If the weather is bad or conditions are bad, they coax people to come because "any day on the mountain is better than a day at the office".

This kind of communication is disingenuous and annoying. Show your audience the respect they deserve. Be real and show the downside as well as the upside. Be transparent. Your audience can see right through your falsely optimistic messages. (We'll get to transparency soon!)

> Be of actual service, not lip service.

Be of actual service, not lip service. It might cost you in the short term, as we might decide not to ski that day, but we'll love you forever for it.

## Story prompts

When you look at your own work, the red flag to watch for is jargon and words with little real meaning or that could mean many things to many people. When you see these popping up, it's an invitation to stop and ask how you might better communicate this message by showing instead of telling.

# How can we shift perceptions about us?

A relationship has begun. You've focused your message, underscored important ideas, and used real words. Connecting can be tenuous and, try as you might, sometimes people just don't get you. How can you break through?

Gaining visibility is often the big challenge, but it doesn't end there. Once they've heard of you, they might not get you. Maybe they don't agree with what you do, or have been misinformed. How can we shift their perception? By telling stories that prove otherwise.

Jane Goodall says that when she is faced with someone who disagrees or objects, she chooses not to get "holier than thou". Confronting and adversarial conversations don't work. Instead, she connects through story.

## Story type: The myth buster

The power of story lets you show instead of tell. Want people to know something about you? It's much easier to show them either directly through your actions or indirectly with your stories of those actions.

Say you are a healthcare clinic working with clients and patients across the healthcare landscape, including self-insured, self-pay, uninsured, veterans, and children. Because you have a division that serves the underserved, you have a high incidence of individuals struggling with substance abuse, and you have become known for that.

But that's not what you *want* to be known for.

What do you do? You don't just come out and say, "Hey, we aren't just for people who struggle with substance abuse." You tell the stories you want people to know. Privacy laws permitting, you show the children and the veterans you've helped.

The best way to debunk myths is to flood the landscape with stories that prove otherwise. It's the same with online reputation management. If a restaurant gets a negative article or review, they simply ask many people to write a positive review and sink the negative with the volume of the positive.

I love the TikTok meme that was popular in 2022. It said, "Tell me about a time you XYZ without saying XYZ." One woman posted, "Tell me your husband won't cheat on you without telling me he won't cheat on you", and proceeded to show a video of him in his underwear, looking out the window and pointing at birds in fascination while talking about them in great detail.

Another said, "Tell me you're the youngest child without telling me you're the youngest child". She showed a photo album containing one photo—her baby picture.

These stories show instead of tell. It's the perfect exercise next time you want to tell someone something you can't say about yourself.

A client in a manufacturing business wanted to differentiate himself as someone who truly cared about the outcomes for his clients, who solved problems and created relationships. It was the ideal time to say he was client-focused. But saying you are client-focused is lip service and that won't do. Being in service does.

How could we tell a story instead? I asked him to tell me about a time he was client-focused without telling me he was client-focused. He described how his customers come to him frustrated that their technology isn't working. Their huge investment is wasted because the software isn't doing what it should be doing. Other vendors have tried but can't seem to fix the issue. They insist that what the clients are asking for can't be done.

They are transactional. Joe's company isn't like that. He said, "We find workarounds and solutions." So we made the headline of his story, "Let's see what's possible." This line opened the door to sharing stories that showed them finding creative solutions to client requests and challenges.

Joe loved the headline because it was the opposite of what his clients were used to hearing.

Do I make it sound too simple? Entire books and bodies of work are dedicated to reputation management. It's not quite as simple as telling a story, but that's a big part and a healthy start to get back on track and become known for what you want to be known for.

## Story prompts

What quality or characteristic do you want people to associate with you? Tell us about a time you were that, without saying you were that.

What do people get wrong about you? What's a story that shows the opposite?

# How best can I communicate a difficult message?

Clarity is the pathway to creating a deep understanding of who you are and what you do. Use stories as a metaphor for your idea. Use precise language, keep your message focused, and expand on a word to get specific and highlight an important idea.

You've established your credibility as a person through stories of your experiences. You've deepened the understanding of your organization and your work through clear and specific messages. What could go wrong?

No one is perfect. Things will go wrong, and you'll have to manage negative or challenging situations. Change-making leaders know what objections might be on the minds of the people they need to reach, and they address those topics actively and transparently.

I had a call with the leader of an organization in which the marketplace had lost trust. (I've changed the details to protect the confidentiality of our conversation.) The leader was an interim CEO who stepped in after the previous leader had been ousted due to questionable fiscal management. It was a high-profile situation that ended up in national news. Revenue had dropped significantly. We had a lengthy discussion on rebuilding trust and getting back on track.

The company's advisory council wanted the new CEO to rebuild trust without talking about "the incident". They contended that they shouldn't draw attention to something people might not already know about. In other words, they wanted to ignore the situation and hope it would go away.

I helped the CEO find middle ground.

## Story type: The elephant

Trust is vital in today's marketplace, but it is hard to earn and easy to lose. Once lost, it's even more difficult to regain. I understand the reluctance to talk about something that hurt your reputation. But the risk is that people will find out later if you hide or ignore it. They may feel deceived, and the spiral of lost trust will continue.

How would it feel to proactively get in front of an issue? In most cases, your audience will appreciate the candor, and you will earn their trust.

This is a complex issue without a right or wrong answer; organizations must weigh what's right for their greater good. You can't ignore the elephant in the room; it's too conspicuous. Yet organizations often pretend not to see it, hoping no one will notice if they avoid the topic.

If you don't tell the stories or address the tough topics, people will make up their own stories. Rather than fret about shining a light on something people otherwise don't know, be far more worried about what stories they will create if you don't give them the truth. Remember the manager I mentioned in the introduction who said that when they don't hear from leadership, they assume they are busy dealing with a lawsuit? Humans have wonderful imaginations.

Do a risk-benefit analysis, of course, but land on the side of transparency to build trust.

It's a vulnerable place, and having the courage to be vulnerable might be one of the biggest barriers to developing a storytelling habit. Will people accept us? Will they even care? We'll talk more about vulnerability in the next section.

Being real asks us to be transparent. No one has patience for couched language or skirting a situation. Give your audience the respect they want and deserve.

When we sit in curiosity, we know what's being said about us. We're asking questions, seeking feedback, and monitoring social media. We know what's happening. There is great power in showing that you know what is being said and addressing it head-on. The power of story allows us to defuse a hot wire.

Being real is vulnerable. Sometimes, it can take you to hell and back.

Hell's Backbone Grill & Farm (HBG) is a stunning farm-to-table restaurant in Boulder, Utah, situated in the most remote small town in the lower 48. It is truly a destination restaurant, and how it can be successful in that remote location is an interesting story in itself. Consistently recognized by chef and food connoisseur James Beard as one of the top restaurants in the country, Jen and Blake were finalists for best chefs in the mountain region by the James Beard Awards for the 2020 season and semi-finalists for Best Chefs in the Southwest in 2017, 2018, and 2019.

The *New Yorker* magazine took note and covered their vocal fight over then-President Trump's plan to reduce the size of the Bears Ears and Escalante National Monuments.[27] (Their restaurant is situated on a piece of land in the Escalante National Monument.)

Jen Castle and Blake Spalding had a difficult decision to make, which unknowingly would determine the survival or failure of their restaurant. Should they or should they not share the dire circumstances of their restaurant with their beloved community?

At the end of 2022, the restaurant was struggling. COVID had had a huge impact, and they had racked up debt to keep their doors open. Several other factors made them realize they would have to close their doors forever. But people close in their circle didn't want to see that happen and urged them to "let the people know".

So, in November 2022, they sent out an email. Here's a snippet:

"Last month, when we sent a newsletter sharing our struggles, we were pretty sure our next letter would include the very sad announcement that we'd be closing our doors. But then you flooded our inboxes with love and encouragement, and when we expressed doubts about the future of HBG, the resounding response we got from so many of you was: 'Don't make this decision without us'."[28]

The email went on to outline three critical needs and how much each would cost. (Debt repayment, a forever home for the restaurant, and infrastructure tune-up.) Each item included a paragraph explaining why and how they got there.

In December 2022, they followed up with another email.:

"When we launched the GoFundMe, we knew, of course, that we had an exceptionally loving and supportive community, but we were completely shocked when our initial goal of $324,000—an auspicious number, a symbolic starting point, and an amount we felt would alleviate our immediate challenges and ensure our short-term survival—was met in under a week. We remain in a state of astonishment, because even after meeting the goal, many of you are continuing to contribute to the fundraiser. This ongoing help is extremely supportive. With every additional donation that comes in, we're able to take a deeper collective breath and envision solutions for a host of complex, longstanding problems. Every contribution helps pave a brighter future for us and our team."

A for-profit restaurant starts a GoFundMe account and raises $400,000 within a month. What's the secret?

When they first announced, via email, the struggles they were facing, they weren't asking for help (yet). They were being transparent, and were getting ready to let go of their beloved restaurant. It takes vulnerability to make the quiet things loud. It connects people to you. That's what made some people respond with words of support and led them to believe doing a GoFundMe was a good idea.

"Of all the hard things we've done (and let's be clear, we have done a lot of very freaking hard things), asking for help in this way might be the very hardest. But we've come to the understanding, at last, that this isn't just about us. Hell's Backbone Grill and Farm is also about you. It always has been."

Make no mistake; there was a great deal of trust and community already built long before the situation came to this. Don't be misled into thinking that transparency will get you this kind of response. It's a storytelling habit over time, that creates relationships built on trust and understanding, with a foundation of having provided an amazing experience to people.

I can personally attest to having one of the loveliest birthday evenings ever at HBG. We bought the cookbook; we follow them on all their socials. We love their story. People love being connected to a purpose, and when you do that—and show vulnerability—they will show up for you. And you, too, will be astonished.

> ## Story prompts
>
> Please note: this section does not constitute any form of legal advice. I am assuming that your "elephant" is legal!
>
> Given that, ask yourself the following questions.
>
> What's your version of the elephant?
>
> What's keeping you up at night?
>
> Where have you lost trust?
>
> Do the risk-benefit analysis before you decide to talk about it. In other words, does it make sense to get ahead of it and build trust and credibility? Or is it best to let it fade away?
>
> What do people get wrong about you?
>
> What stories can you tell that debunk those misperceptions or misunderstandings?

When Jane Goodall said, "When we get to the heart with story, we may not know it at the time but people will go on thinking", she confirmed that storytelling is more effective than debating.

Tell stories that prove the truth. Don't try to argue. When you deliver difficult messages, you show the real you. That attracts the right people.

## Real is the story of you

Being real is tricky, and I ask you to do so with care, as it is subjective. If you take my suggestion literally, you might not do your hair in the morning. Heck, you might stop grooming altogether because you are who you are, not who others think you should be.

There's a caveat, though: being yourself isn't always the best thing. That was apparent in BP CEO Tony Hayward's inadvertent moment of authenticity during the 2010 Gulf oil spill. In an interview, his admission, "I just want my life back", ignited an uproar because some of his employees had just lost their lives.[29] In some people, the real them are massive jerks.

Let's assume that's not you. Generally, you are a good and well-intentioned person with stories to share of your mistakes, foibles, and transformations. You are far more than the highlight reels of your social media presence.

These are stories that others can connect to. There is a depth of perception that inexplicably attracts people who want to be a part of you, your team, and your business. And the stories of you, your work, proactively acknowledging the potentially detractive or negative perceptions, being in service rather than indulgent.

The real you is relatable. Let's keep going. We're on a roll now.

# 10

# MAKE IT RELATABLE

## Balance the energy

Being relatable is about meeting your audience where they are—not where *you* are. People act on things and people they understand. Like a power converter, we need to match the energy level to the energy source.

At its highest level of abstraction, relatability is about cracking open for others to see what's inside, so they can sort through and take in what they want and need. If you've ever bought a gadget in plastic clamshell packaging, you've experienced the frustration of removing the contents. It's smooth and shiny and impossible to get into.

The inside, the contents—that's the real stuff. That plastic clamshell gatekeeps the contents. If only there were a pull tab option to open it. That pull tab is relatability. It's the small bit about you or your company that gives someone the option to say, "Yeah, I want what's inside". They pull on the tab because you've provided it.

In this section, we'll talk about getting personal and emotional.

Yes, I want you to talk about feelings. And yes, it comes with risk. And you have to be OK with the idea that your story will not be for everyone. We'll also look at how to create understanding by changing the story you tell around the problem you solve (and the solution). Lastly, to be relatable, we have to help people who aren't directly impacted by your idea to understand it within their frame of reference.

Relatable leaders:

- get personal and show they care
- match the story to the need
- make global ideas local.

## What's your story?

Change-making leaders take small risks in their storytelling that make them vulnerable and, therefore, relatable.

In 2009, my PR agency was struggling in the wake of the recession, so I attended a PR conference to make a plan to rebuild. I felt some shame over my perceived failure and didn't want to draw attention to myself. So, I planned to be a fly on the wall at the event and take in as much information as I could.

As it turned out, the event organizers had something else in mind. In the opening session, first-time attendees were asked to take the stage and introduce themselves. I had to buck up and tell my story, even though I really didn't want to.

I put on my best secure face and gave a quick introduction. I live in Sandpoint, Idaho, and whenever I say Idaho, people automatically assume Boise and tell me about someone they know there. But I live nine hours from Boise via a two-lane winding highway and in a different time zone. So I started my story by saying, "I'm based in Sandpoint, Idaho, which is nowhere near Boise." I then explained my work and specialty areas and thought that would be the end of it. But it wasn't.

For the following days, people sought me out to speak to me. They remembered me, especially the Idaho part, and some were even envious of my work.

What I thought wasn't very interesting, they found fascinating. What I wanted to keep hidden was the very thing people connected with. These relationships later proved to be highly influential. Years later, I became a leader in the organization that planned the event and handled the Connect 101 part of the session!

The power of telling our story is that we attract the right people. Not everyone sought me out. (Your story is not for everyone.) That can be hard to accept because it takes some vulnerability to share your story, knowing that you risk rejection.

Getting personal means you shouldn't take it personally when your story isn't for them. It vets the others pretty quickly. Wish them well and carry on.

Snowbird Ski Resort in Utah embraces this idea. In an ad campaign in the late 2010s, they ran two-page ads in SKI Magazine highlighting the one-star reviews they received. To give you some context, Snowbird is known for some of the best powder skiing in the world. They are not known for groomed runs, which appeal to beginner and intermediate skiers. The following image was one of the reviews they featured.[30]

The photo shows an advanced skier deep in champagne powder. Snowbird understands the assignment. They celebrate people who do like their stories and are coming to get more. The "Disappointed" person who left this review is not a skier who will like Snowbird.

Focus on where you are accepted, who you are and what you stand for. You cannot be uniquely loved if you try to be universally liked.

Change-making leaders get personal. Who you are is fundamental to any transformational idea because people will want to relate to and know you before they learn from you or do what you ask.

## Story type: Your "why" story

The most obvious personal story is your "why" story.

One of my favorite "why" stories is that of Bobby Mann, chief programs officer of the Humane Rescue Alliance. On a Zoom call, when everyone was asked to introduce themselves, Bobby turned a potential yawn moment into a memorable one. After he told his story, I could only think, "Wow, I want to work with him." Here's my paraphrase of Bobby's story.

"I was studying to become a fashion designer. In school, I couldn't get any dates. One day, I went for a walk, and a man on the street was offering a dog up for adoption. Concerned for the dog's future, I adopted the puppy and soon had many dates. That was when I knew I wanted to go into animal welfare."

What about you? Why do you do the work you do? Think of your story as a moment or a time that inspired you to do this work, not as a chronology. Remember, a story is not a history.

Your "why" could be something that happened after you started doing the work. Or maybe you do your work because you have a young child at home for whom you want to provide a stable future. Our lives are not grand designs, and we don't have to pretend they are. You may very well be in a job because it was the first interview you secured or perhaps because it's a practice inherited from your family.

We are not here to fabricate masterful stories. The simplest stories can touch our hearts. And everyone has a story to tell.

> ## Story prompts
>
> When did you decide to do what you do?
>
> If you landed in this work by accident rather than design, what made you realize you want to stay?
>
> What are you most proud of about what you do?
>
> What mistake have you made, or big lesson learned?
>
> What is life teaching you at this moment?

## What's the best way to move your audience?

"Emotion is the glue that connects storyteller and listeners," wrote Meg Bowles and Catherine Burns in *How to Tell a Story*.[31] Emotion is contagious, so it's one of the best ways to move your audience. Yes, it's risky and it can also be highly rewarding.

The TV series *Ted Lasso* is a massive hit, even though soccer isn't currently a mainstream sport here in the US.[32] The stories are of love and redemption, friendships forged on the field, in the locker room, and outside the game, of losing games, training hard, and winning. These are themes everyone can relate to and aspire to.

Our stories set us apart, but our emotions bring us together.

A story without emotion is like Google Maps without the terrain layer turned on. It's flat with some lines but no contours. There's no texture, and it's missing a lot of detail. You see the landscape but can't really get a sense of what it's like.

To *evoke* emotion from your audience, you must *invoke* emotion. Turn the terrain layer on. A simple way to do this is by describing how the characters in the story feel.

A single mom recounted the story of escaping her abusive husband with their two daughters. She was strong, intelligent, and courageous in sharing her story to raise funds for the shelter that helped her. Her story highlighted the events as they unfolded without emotion.

The story had people on the edges of their seats. But everyone had one question because it wasn't an experience they'd had or could relate to. They wanted to know, "What was it like?" What was it like to drive across the country for two days with two young girls in baby seats in the back of the car? What was it like at the last gas station where she spent her last bit of cash to fill up her car? What was it like when she knew she could drive no further and would have to find a place to stay?

She told the audience the stories she recounted to her girls during the drive to keep their spirits up and make it seem like a game despite her fear of being caught by her husband. She told us about the 76 phone calls she made at that last gas station parking lot until she found a place that could provide shelter for her and her kids so they could get on their feet. More than the events, it was the emotion that brought the audience to their feet at the end of her story.

Experiences are unique, while emotions are universal.

## Story type: show how much you care

It takes courage to talk about feelings. Leaders often worry that it shows weakness, but, in truth, it's the opposite. Feelings show strength, particularly when you need to connect and relate to people. They want to know you have feelings, too. You're just like them!

A company I worked with was called out by a major social media influencer for a pattern of harm to their LBGTQIA employees (some of the details in this story have been altered to protect privacy). Employees (not to mention customers and partners) looked to the leader for their response. The CEO drafted a response for my feedback. It was good. It took the matter seriously, addressed everything being done to repair this harm, and explained what they would do to keep it from happening in the future. It was good, but it wasn't great.

Reading it through the lens of the customer or employee didn't make me feel like this call-out mattered to the CEO. I didn't get any connection, just a well-written apology. It could be better.

What caused the lack of connection? There was no emotion. It was a matter-of-fact statement.

I asked the CEO how he *felt* about the situation. He said that it upset him, as a gay man, that employees were experiencing something he'd had to endure with another employer. He vowed this wouldn't be the case on his watch.

That was it! Why not tell this story? Why not add even this brief statement to the story? He told me people didn't care how he felt; they just wanted him to fix the problem.

But people *do* care about how you feel.

Knowing how you feel creates common ground because we all have feelings.

Connection is not about finding common ground. The *Ted Lasso* series is not about soccer; it's about overcoming hurdles. Emotions are universal, and they create connection.

Back to the CEO. The new policies they are deploying in response to the situation are important. For someone in the affected community to state that he is appalled that others would feel harmed by policies would be powerful. To empathize and say, "I remember when I was in your position, supervising a small team with big dreams, and a time I was [fill in your story here]", shows you care deeply and that you will fix it.

Are you still worried that your vulnerability shows weakness or admits wrongdoing? David Calhoun, CEO of Boeing, didn't hesitate when a door plug on a 737 Max 9 jet blew out in mid-air over Oregon in January 2024. Miraculously, the seat next to the blowout was empty, and no one was injured. The plane made a safe emergency landing, but it was traumatizing for all involved.

Calhoun acknowledged the gravity of the situation and that a mistake was made, although what mistake exactly they didn't know (and still don't as I write this). In an internal memo to his staff, Calhoun wrote, "…we're starting from a very anxious moment with our customers, and we simply have to deal with that reality. So it's going to be a lot about transparency." He described how the event impacted him. In his public statement, he said he was "shaken to the bone", devastated and emotional when he saw the video of the incident.[33]

If you think people don't care about you, you're right. They don't. They care about how you can help them. They care that you see and understand, and care about what matters to them. They care that you are the right person to associate with. And they can't make that determination if they don't know what you care about.

Infusing the experience of you with little things about you helps them get that understanding.

We want to know that you, as a leader, care. That this truly matters to you. People do care about how you feel *and* they want you to fix it. The two are not mutually exclusive. Remember, to evoke emotion in your audience, you must invoke emotion. The details of the stories vary, but the emotions are what everyone relates to.

### Story prompts

How did the character in the story feel before, during, and after the event?

What was it like for them?

What did they learn that others can benefit from?

## Why can't we get attention for our work?

I hear this so often that it's the underlying premise of this whole book. How do we get people to pay attention to what we care about?

The answer? It's a noisy world, and there are so many possible things for your audience to care about. You have to stand out to get their attention.

The problem is in what story you are offering. Are your stories about the solution you provide or the problem you solve? Which do you think will make people listen with heart?

## Story type: The problem you solve, not the solution you provide

Change-making leaders meet people where they are by matching the story to the need in the conversation. Your core competency is at the heart of your stories. What you are good at is the thing you do, and the message you want to share with others to get them to say "Yes" to you, to choose you. Your competency solves a problem. There are two parts here: the problem (the why) and the solution (the impact). Why it matters and what it does.

From why to impact, your story changes based on where people are on the journey to get to know you. Let me explain.

We tend to talk about our work from our own perspective and priorities, not those of the people we want to reach. Consider that every human walking the planet has a similar but different thought bubble over their head.

What's in those thought bubbles?

A: The Weber Grill salesperson: I need to sell these barbecue grills.

B: The home chef: I wish I could cook steak better.

A: The caseworker for the state child welfare department: We need more foster parents to help these children in need.

B: The potential foster parent: I need more purpose in my life.

A: The communications person for the vet hospital: How can we raise awareness around this cutting-edge canine arthroscopic procedure?

B: The dog owner: My dog has hip pain and won't lie down.

Can you see how each scenario reflects a potential disconnect between the teller and the listener. Our priorities misalign because the teller is focused on their solution and the receiver has their own problem.

Take the first example. The home chef wants to be a better cook and make a better steak. But we're focused on selling grills, so we're shouting, "Check out these great grills at great prices!" Like balloons on strings above our heads, those thought bubbles bounce off each other, unmatched and unresolved. You remain ignored and misunderstood while they have an unresolved problem or unanswered question.

In the second example, if your job was to recruit and retain foster parents, would you put up a sign or a social media post that said, "Foster parents needed!" Or would you say something about finding more purpose in life by helping a child who needs love?

To create a deeper understanding of who you are and the work you do, we have to get out of our heads and into theirs. You have solutions and want to talk about them. They have problems but may not know a solution is available, so they aren't even looking for you.

I know this last example all too well, as my dog, Jackson, had chronic hip pain. Things came to a head one evening when he was in such pain that he couldn't lie down. I did what any caring parent would do and turned to the internet to find a solution, typing "pain management for chronic canine hip dysplasia" in the search bar. At the top of the results was a story about a man with a dog with a similar problem. He found help at a vet hospital not far from my home that performed a procedure called arthroscopic surgery to remove bone fragments in his dog's knees. It turned out that Jackson was a great candidate for this, and he had the surgery within a few weeks. His pain was successfully managed.

If the story had been about arthroscopic surgery, I would have scrolled past it because I had no idea what it was or that it would help. But the story was about helping dogs with chronic pain, so our thought bubbles merged. I gave them a bunch of money. They gave my dog a new lease on life.

Purpose-driven, passionate, and knowledgeable people that we are, we tend to talk about what's on *our* minds, not what is on *their* minds. We forget that our priority isn't their priority.

What's on *our* minds is often the solution we provide. What's on *their* mind is the problem they have.

We create understanding by meeting people where they are: in their problem set, not in the solution.

When we don't do this, our message falls flat, and we wonder why. It's frustrating. To meet people where they are requires successfully answering the questions and concerns on their minds.

You're right if you think that not everyone searches based on their problems. Once they have heard of you and understand your solution, they have new questions requiring new stories. For example, maybe, after learning about arthroscopic surgery, I read about its associated risks. Maybe I'd check the reputation of the doctors who do the surgery. As your audience progresses on the journey to get to know you, they vet the solution. New questions will require you to add more stories to the conversation.

You have more than one story to tell.

## Story prompts

What problem do you solve?

What's the story around that problem? How do people experience it?

What solution do you offer, and how does it work?

What doubts might they have about you? What doubts might they have about your solution?

What do others say about your solution?

The story you tell changes to meet people where they are. Sometimes, there is a great physical or psychological distance between your idea and where those people are.

## What if they think our work doesn't impact them?

Change-makers make global ideas local. When your message or idea is far removed from what people know and understand, we can use story to bridge that gap and help them understand from within their frame of reference.

Maybe you are trying to explain a complex and technical concept or working to fix a wicked problem on the other side of the world. When your story is so far removed from the listener's lived experience, it's helpful to translate it into their experience and bring the idea into their proximity.

Who owns a story once it's been told? Once a story has been told, the receiver makes of it what they will. They receive it through the lens of their perspective.

The philosopher Aristotle wrote, "All storytelling is a kind of imitation."[34] It is a representation of what we know. Even the most imaginative story reflects the world as we know it. Otherwise, no one would be able to relate to it. A good storyteller understands this and helps the audience understand from within their frame of reference.

The questions you want to answer are: what do they need to know to understand the concept? And, most importantly, why should they care? How does it impact them?

There are a few ways to deepen understanding. Find a metaphor, speak their language, and help them experience the idea. Let's explore each of these.

## Story type: The analogy

An analogy or a metaphor uses a common object or idea to represent an unrelated concept. A story can act as a symbol for an unrelated concept. We can help people make sense of mind-numbing numbers, statistics or abstract concepts by making them imaginable in their context.

In Chapter 19, I wrote about using story as a metaphor to help you communicate a complex message. Karishma Polwar used tomato soup to help us understand oil. This is the same idea, but it bears repeating, so I'll share one more example.

A single mom I worked with used the image of a bubble to help her young daughter process the fear she was experiencing as they drove across the country to a new place. She told her daughter, "This is a normal feeling when you are outside your comfort zone. It is like a bubble around your body, and, right now, the bubble is really close. We just need to blow air into it to make it bigger." Every now and then in the following days, she'd see her daughter blowing into an imaginary straw.

Such images can make the unfamiliar familiar, making your audience more likely to remember your message.

## Story prompts

Think about what your audience knows, understands, and values. What in their world relates to your message? How can you use that to shine a light on your idea?

# How do I choose the right words for impact?

Words matter, and when you speak their language, people get it.

Language separates humans from other species because it allows us to teach and pass on knowledge. We can speak of things that aren't present. Words give us the ability to talk about events in the past and learn from them. As Jane Goodall explains, language means we can plan for the future and discuss ideas, bouncing them back and forth to share the accumulated wisdom of an entire group.[35]

We take language for granted. It is very powerful—so much so that it literally affects what we see. Russians see eight colors in the rainbow when most of us only see seven. Is that because Russians have better vision than us? No. It's because they have two words for blue.[36] When your idea is geographically or psychologically distant from the people you want to reach, framing the idea in their language will matter.

## Story model: Use their language

If you are presenting to a group for significant funding, speak their language so they can see a way to support your idea.

The narrative was simple when my client, a conservation organization in Jackson Hole, Wyoming, presented to a committee for a $750,000 grant. Over-visitation of their open spaces was threatening the wildlife, the forest, and the humans. The solution was a program to teach visitors to recreate responsible recreation. In preparation for the presentation, we researched the members of the voting committee to understand what each individual cared about and where their priorities were.

For example, one of the members was a hotel executive. What's in his thought bubble? "How can I get more heads in beds?" We needed to show how our objectives aligned and tell the story in their frame of reference. If a disaster, such as a wildfire, were to hit the area, the very thing people were coming to visit would be gone. No more heads in beds. That sounds easy, but we took it one step further and rather than talking about the surrounding forest as a natural resource, we called it an asset. The narrative highlighted the idea of protecting the asset, which in turn would bring people to the destination. The group received all the votes (including from the hotel executive) and was fully funded.

This may sound like a minor change, but we made sure to speak the language of hotel executives so they could understand why they should support an initiative that ostensibly didn't impact them.

## Story prompts

What industry or sector-related language does your audience use?

What is the key concern or priority in their mind? How can you reduce psychological or geographic distance and bridge it with their language?

## Story type: Visualization

Another beautiful way to bring distant ideas close to the listener, psychologically or physically, is to help them see your messages.

Paint a picture so eloquently that you bring it into their world.

One of the most powerful ways to get people to care about something is to help them experience it.

That is how Canyonlands National Park, Utah, came to be. In *Erosion: Essays of Undoing,* Terry Tempest Williams recounts how a flight and expedition through the wilderness of Utah with a group of congressmen and journalists was pivotal in establishing the national park which many wanted to keep unprotected for mining, grazing, and commercial development.[37]

In 1961, the Secretary of Interior to President John F. Kennedy, Stewart Udall, envisioned the national park and organized a five-day tour of the region with 30 people, including photographers, writers, and senators, to see the land for themselves. Everyone was awestruck by its beauty, and the park was established, despite compromises.

In another case, Operation Smile works in remote villages across the world to give children with cleft conditions a chance at life.[38] This situation is far removed from the ordinary every day of most potential donors, so they created an experience for visitors to its global headquarters in Virginia Beach.

Their Interactive Learning Center takes visitors on the journey of a child affected by cleft conditions so they can experience it firsthand. The guide begins by assigning you the identity of a child whom the organization has helped. They even hand you a mock passport in that child's name. Throughout the tour, you carry the passport and learn the child's story and where they live. As you go, the guide presents you with the question of how to reach children with cleft conditions in remote villages.

From the room hung with images of the village where "your child" lives, you turn the corner and are transported to the small family's outdoor kitchen and living quarters. You experience their living conditions and see what they see when they first learn of the screening opportunity available for their child. As you leave the hut, you board a bus that takes you to the clinic. You see what a screening area looks like, what happens when a child doesn't meet the criteria and eligibility for the surgery, how they help that child meet those requirements and finally, what the surgical and recovery rooms look like.

The rich storytelling of this experience can't help but fill you with compassion. I imagine it's a similar feeling of awe that those senators and journalists experienced in 1961 in Utah.

This kind of storytelling may feel out of reach. You don't have the budget to take a group of individuals on an expedition or the generosity of a donor who funded the Interactive Learning Center at Operation Smile.

You don't have to. The idea is to bring something outside your listener's world into their world. How can you help them experience the thing within their reference?

> ## Story prompt
>
> I call it "Imagine if...".
>
> To help you understand this exercise, here's an example:
>
> When the Taliban seized control of Afghanistan in 2021, millions of Afghans fled the country. Narges Nazif, an Afghan woman in Seattle, helped Americans understand their plight. This was an important story to be told, particularly in small towns, where residents grappled with the uncertainty and the controversy of welcoming these people to their communities. Nazif wrote, "... just imagine yourself leaving the house every morning thinking about what if it's your last goodbye with your loved ones. Yes, this is almost every Afghan's story. Living in a safe and peaceful environment is every human being's right, but not everyone is lucky or privileged."[39]

## Story model: Walk in their shoes

Empathy goes in both directions. To help someone understand your world, you have to know theirs. If you want to get to the heart with a story and change minds and behaviors, consider why they would care to do so. Creating understanding and relatability doesn't have to cost millions of dollars. It starts by reflecting on what the conversation needs from you. Why should your audience care? How can they understand it better? How can you meet them where they are to achieve a mutually beneficial outcome?

As change-making leaders, it helps to set aside our priorities and speak to theirs. Paint a picture if you can't take them there. Bring an example of the greater idea or concept to life with a story. Make it an experience.

> ### Story prompts
>
> Finding the metaphor: Thinking about the message you want to communicate, where does the concept exist elsewhere? This "elsewhere" should be near the people you want to reach—a place they can understand.
>
> Why should they care if they believe it doesn't directly affect them?
>
> How can you help them see that it might impact them?
>
> How can you help them experience it?

## Relatable is the story of you and them

People act on things and people they understand and that are familiar. If you remain closed off like the plastic clamshell packaging, it's too difficult for them to get to the contents to build trust and decide to buy from you, work with you, or give to you.

Consider how you can bring your essence into the experience of you. You are correct in thinking there is a risk there. Not everyone will be attracted to your story or to you, but don't take it personally because you will attract the right people. How lovely will it be to work with people who accept you for who you are?

Beyond you personally, how can people deeply grasp the work you do? Some are looking for a solution to a problem—without knowing what the solution might look like. Meet their thought bubble with your stories about the problem. They will go into vetting mode once they know about you and the solution you offer. They will research your solution by asking others and reading articles. What questions are on their minds before they decide? How do your stories demystify your work?

Being relatable means we show our human side, our less-than-perfect side. We take time to meet our audience where they are because we know they hear and consume stories from the lens of their perspective and their structured belief system. Use analogies, choose your words carefully and paint a picture so others can visualize your ideas.

The story changes; the truth does not.

The power of story is grounded when you are real. It is balanced when you are relatable and meet people where they are. Now, it's time to elevate the energy. It's time to be riveting.

# 11

# MAKE IT RIVETING

## Show people what is possible

The power of story is generative. It radiates from within and lifts everyone up. Riveting storytellers show people a better future which inspires them to action. There is no point in listening to your story if we or the world are not better for it. Possibility is irresistible.

When you're real, you gain credibility. When you're relatable, we get to know and understand you. When you're riveting, you instigate an emotional shift that inspires action. Riveting is like charisma—it gives an exponential boost to the power of being real and relatable.

In this section, we'll explore the key qualities of being riveting: your uniqueness, positivity, and connection to purpose.

What makes one conversation boring and the other riveting?

Riveting stories drown out the noise and distractions because they help us to stand out instead of fitting in. We become the "one and only" in your market. People refer you and the choice to work with you is easy. This is the emotional shift that is not based on cost. It's relational, not transactional.

Riveting leaders:

- stand out instead of blending in
- have a growth mindset
- articulate a vision.

In this section, we'll explore what it takes to differentiate yourself. We'll talk about feelings. Yes, I want you to talk about feelings!

We have agreed in previous pages that you shouldn't be the star of your story. In this section, we'll see what happens when you tell other people's stories and when you take a stand about something potentially polarizing. We'll learn how to tell the bigger story so we can spark imagination and get people to think, talk, and act.

But first, have you stepped into your truth? How can I/we differentiate ourselves?

## Story type: Brand You

Change-making leaders stand out instead of blending in. When we try to fit in or be how we think we should be, we tend to hold our stories (and our true selves) back. That's too bad because our stories are the very thing that make us memorable and create connection. Instead of showing up as you think you should, what would happen if you showed showed up as the person you could be? The one you want to be?

Change-makers are riveting because they show up, comfortable with who they are and don't feel compelled to be someone they are not.

Vivian Morris may be fictional, but she is real, relatable, and entirely riveting. As the main character in Elizabeth Gilbert's novel *City of Girls,* we can learn from Vivian's journey to find herself because she is in all of us.[40] The following excerpts are from the perspective of an elderly Vivian, with the advantage of wisdom and hindsight of her coming of age in the 1940s and 1950s New York City theater district.

On finding her way:

"I didn't understand what I was doing at college, aside from fulfilling a destiny whose purpose nobody had bothered explaining to me. From earlier childhood, I'd been told that I would attend Vassar, but nobody had told me why."

Someone (her parents) told Vivian how life should be, and she went along with it because she was young and didn't know any other, or better, way.

Are you a leader asking your people to do things without helping them to understand why?

Or are you in Vivian's shoes, following rules that don't make sense? Are you obeying rules that don't fit with who you are or want to be?

When Vivian's parents lost hope in their daughter, they shipped her off to New York City to live with her aunt, who owned a theater. There, Vivian was introduced to a life she could align with, one that at the time was considered scandalous because it simply wasn't how women should behave.

Vivian never married. She started her own business and (gasp!) slept with men as she pleased.

"...if you're wondering whether I ever had crises of conscience about my promiscuity, I can honestly tell you: no. I did believe that my behaviors made me unusual—because it didn't seem to match the behavior of other women—but I didn't believe that it made me bad. I used to think that I was bad, mind you, but by the time the war ended, I was finished with all that. The war had invested me with an understanding that life is both dangerous and fleeting, and thus there is no point in denying yourself pleasure or adventure while you are here.

"...at some point in a woman's life, she just gets tired of being ashamed all the time. After that, she is free to become whoever she truly is."

We are all told stories when we are young, and those stories shape the stories we tell ourselves. We then experience the shame of not living up to those stories. Instead, my hope is that we can edit our stories. We all have agency but may not realize that until later in life. What if we decided now to write our own stories?

It's about giving ourselves permission, without waiting for others to step into leadership of our lives and our stories. We are self-determining individuals who decide how we want to live and how we want to lead.

Vivian's friend Frank declares:

"The world ain't straight. You grow up thinking things are a certain way. You think there are rules. You think there's a way that things have to be. You try to live straight. But the world doesn't care about your rules, or what you believe. The world ain't straight, Vivian.... Our rules, they don't mean a thing. The world just happens to you sometimes, is what I think. And people just gotta keep moving through it, best they can."

If we adhere too strongly to the rules and what should be, we hold back on our stories, the very stories that allow us to stand out, be memorable, and change the world.

Your uniqueness makes you riveting and it's time to embrace it. A million people might do what you do, but not a single person shares the stories you are developing throughout the journey of this book. It's time to find your voice and step into the spotlight.

What are you holding back because you are working hard to fit in?

For decades, I straightened and colored my hair because I thought my messy silver curls made me look old and I wasn't polished and professional enough. I felt like I needed to show up as someone I wasn't. Once I let my real self show, I don't necessarily love it more, but others do. I get compliments almost every day from complete strangers. No one ever noticed my hair before. Lest you think this is a superficial story about my hair, it's anything but. This is about feeling the need to fit in and what happens when you stop being who you should be and start being who you are. And, how it changes the way you show up.

In the Real section, you thought about your story as a biography. In Relatable, you explored your "why" story. There is far more to you than just those stories, of course. The stories of your personal experience and expertise are a great source and offer tiny handholds. When you infuse your personality into your work, you begin to develop Brand You.

> ## Story prompts
>
> Note three things that immediately come to mind in answering the following questions:
>
> What do you love?
>
> What do you care about?

Try a free-form thinking exercise and write the answers to these questions. Don't overthink it. There is no right and wrong. Maybe you love watching your kids at a soccer game. Did something happen last week at the soccer game? A conversation in the stands? Or a lesson your kid learned that relates to something happening at work? Bring that into your professional life. You don't have to share more than you are comfortable with, and you don't have to go on and on about soccer.

The story isn't about soccer. It could be about resilience on the field or how you had a disagreement with another parent and were able to resolve it. The story focuses on them, but in so doing, you've opened a window to who you are.

How can you bring these things into the experience of you? Here are a few examples of how others have done it.

A conference speaker at an SEO conference was one of a hundred similar speakers. But he loves movies from the 1980s and used a different '80s movie theme to introduce each of his tips for better SEO. Of all the speakers, he was the most memorable.

The regional manager of a financial services firm told me the most response they have ever received from their monthly client newsletters was a Christmas card with personal photos of all the staff.

I spoke at a conference and the case studies and examples I used were naturally from outdoor brands because it's who I am and what I know. A CEO in the audience hired me because he was an Ironman athlete, and he felt a connection to my stories.

Given a choice, people work with people they relate to. It's natural to do this in conversation, looking for people, locations, and activities in common. What's one of the first things you do before meeting someone new? Check their LinkedIn profile to learn about them and to see if you share any connections, locations, or schools.

You might choose your financial advisor or physician based on their lifestyle match with yours. Having things in common is a great starting point.

When you get personal, you create an opportunity to let someone know you. If they choose, they can say, "My kid is a soccer player too. He's going to State Championships." You can see what happens from there. A conversation ensues with an opportunity to deepen a relationship by showing curiosity and getting to know each other.

Don't be afraid to bring your essence into the experience of you. These are the optional handholds your audience can pull on to learn more. If nothing else, they help you to be memorable.

You want more than to be memorable, though, right? You want to be *refer-able*. And infusing the story of you into the experience of you is an important start. And there's more.

# How do we get people to refer us?

Asking how to get people to refer you is the wrong question. But I made it the chapter heading because I know it's in your thought bubble. The better question is, "How can I get people to tell our story?" The simple answer to that is to *be* refer-able. *Be* someone people want to talk about.

There is nothing wrong with asking people to refer you and tell your story, but your customers aren't motivated to talk about you unless they love you, and in talking about you, they look better. They don't want a 10% discount to refer you. They want the satisfaction of knowing they made someone else's life better by sharing their knowledge of you.

That means your job is *not* to give out 10% discounts. It's to be real, relatable, and riveting.

There is a great deal of power when someone else tells your story. Trusted outside parties or influencers have more sway over your potential clients. So much is said about you when you aren't in the room. The best way to manage that is to be someone who inspires only positive stories.

When Under Armour's speed suits were blamed for the U.S. speed skating team's poor performance in the 2014 Olympics, the company found itself in a difficult position.[41]

As a U.S. Olympic speed skating sponsor, Under Armour spent a great deal of time and money developing (with aerospace enterprise Lockheed Martin) a high-tech suit to give the U.S. speed skaters a competitive advantage. Race wins come down to mere hundredths of a second, so every detail was carefully tested.

Shani Davis was expected to win gold and came in 8th. No one medaled. And they pointed fingers at the suit for their poor performance. As a result, the U.S. team voted to change speed suits.

It was a nightmare for everyone involved. I watched to see Under Armour's response. First, they said nothing, just stood behind the suits, the research that went into them, and the technology.

I am sure it was tough to stand by while the media (and the team) blamed them for the lack of medals. But what was to be gained by responding and what could they say? That it's not the suit's fault; it's the athlete's? Anything Under Armour could say would come across as defensive and unpatriotic. It's better to say nothing and set about solving the issue than to deflect blame.

When the U.S. team went back to their old, trusted suits, the team's performance did not improve.

When asked if he felt vindicated that the team didn't fare any better when they switched suits, Under Armour CEO Kevin Plank said emphatically, "No. We remain patriots first. As I sit there watching the events on TV and my laptop, I'm wearing red, white, and blue and an American flag."[42]

Kevin Plank exemplified what it means to be someone who *inspires* positive stories, rather than *asking* for them.

When the sponsorship contract came up for renewal, Under Armour not only renewed their sponsorship contract with the U.S.

Speed skating team, they doubled their commitment. Their stock price immediately rose 4%.

Plank's response to his detractors? "We don't want the story going any longer…we want to make sure our message is there that this isn't just a one and done…there is speculation out there about how we are going to react …. We will stand up, and we will come back."

Plank let their actions tell the story and relied (or hoped) that others would fill in the blanks.

Michel Mulder, who led a Dutch sweep of the medals in the men's 500, said of the team and the suits: "It could also be that they (the U.S. team) were just outclassed here."[43]

There you have it. Someone else told the story. Although thoughts like that may have been on the minds of Under Armour, it would have been brand suicide to say it out loud. However, if a competitor wants to say it, far be it for anyone to keep them from speaking their mind!

There is power in having advocates who will defend you without being asked. You can see this at work with your favorite online influencer who might get attacked for something they said or even wore. Their loyal fans will pile on in response.

Your actions influence stories, which influence action. It's up to you to deliver an experience that makes people want to tell your story without being asked. I've no doubt there will have been a time when you loved working with someone so much that you told everyone about it.

## Story type: Be referable

If you want more referrals, be someone who gets referrals. Asking for them is OK, but no one will refer you if you aren't referable. Provide an experience so memorable and so positive, you get talked about all the time. Be referable and you will get referrals.

> ## Story prompts
>
> Who do you trust to tell your story?
>
> How could you ask them without asking?

## Story type: Tell their success stories

So far, in this section, we've made the stories about you and how you stand out instead of blending in. The other thing that differentiates you is the stories of those you've helped. No one else has helped them the way you have.

At its most superficial, these are your success stories. But it's more than that. Their story allows you to shine a light on someone else. The power of riveting stories is exponential—we lift each other up.

Corporate banks get this. Citigroup features stories of their clients that show how Citigroup helps small businesses succeed. Profiling their clients lifts everyone up.

## Story prompts

Show, not boast. Instead of announcing a new client (something PR and advertising agencies love to do), show the problem you solved for an existing client. Sure, do a case study, but make it a story people want to read because they can see themselves in it.

Host a podcast. Interview clients, customers, and people you'd like to work with. Help them share their expertise and best practices, positioning you as the thought leader.

When the vet hospital mentioned earlier told the story of a dog with chronic pain, I recognized what my dog was experiencing. The journey to get to know you can be long, winding, and unpredictable. But in the case of the vet hospital, the journey was only about 10 minutes as I raced to book a consultation. The next day, I spent $4,000 to relieve Jackson's pain. I'd call that a pretty riveting story.

Who have you helped?

Instead of making the story about you, make it about them and how they succeeded (thanks to you, of course).

# What sells better? Hope or doom?

There's a quote attributed to St Augustine that goes, "Hope has two beautiful daughters; their names are Anger and Courage. Anger at the way things are, and Courage to see that they do not remain as they are."

Change-making leaders have both anger and courage. They believe that things can change and are committed to doing so.

What if you have a story no one wants to hear? How can you make it riveting?

There is a buffalo on a ranch I used to drive by almost every day. I can't be sure, but the buffalo seemed sad and lonely. (And yes, a buffalo's resting face tends to be sad and lonely, so I could be making all this up.) The point is, I wish that buffalo was free to roam around and that it had friends.

It's not always there, but on the days I do see it, I look away. Why? Because I don't know what or if there is anything I can do to help it. What would I do? Pull into the ranch and ask to speak to the property owner and ask how he cares for his buffalo? (Tricky, when I don't know the first thing about these matters.) Maybe it doesn't need my help. Maybe on the days I don't see it, it's in another pen frolicking with its girlfriend! Or perhaps its owner is taking it out for a walk.

I look away because I have no understanding of the situation, and I feel helpless to do anything about it.

Homelessness, healthcare equity, animal welfare, and conservation are just four of the many lonely buffalos needing our help and involvement. If we don't give people the information they need to understand the situation or provide small steps and solutions that enable them to be part of the solution, they will look away when we confront them.

These are urgent messages with much at stake, and leaders struggle to find the right balance in delivering the message. They don't want to sound all doom and gloom, but does a positive message drive action?

Studies go both ways on the benefits of positive and negative appeals. It is up to you to decide what works best for your organization.

Some research shows that people are likely to check out over negative messages, while others show they are better at compelling action.[44] Yet another study says negative messages might drive short-term results, but positive messages drive behavioral change over time.[45] It's not cut and dried, so it's up to you to decide what works best. What does your gut say? How do you want to show up? What aligns best with your values?

Perhaps you've tried the optimistic approach and you're not getting traction. If you're thinking your positive message isn't working, get bold. Say or do something to annoy them. Provoke them. Get under their skin. Spark a little anger. But do so with purpose and light the flame that leads to action.

## Story type: Point out progress

Focus on your progress rather than where you are falling short. In their book *10x is Easier than 2x,* Benjamin Hardy and Dan Sullivan explain how focusing on the gain rather than the gap is motivational.[46] When we focus on progress, we provide hope that the outcome is achievable and getting within reach rather than the opposite which can feel hopeless and therefore create apathy.

THE POWER OF STORY

## Story prompt

What's wrong with the situation in question?

Why is this a problem for your audience?

Show the progress and give concrete ways your audience can make an impact.

## Story type: Provoke with purpose

When President Trump attempted to reduce the sizes of two national monuments in Utah, the clothing company Patagonia blacked out its home page and, in huge font, stated:

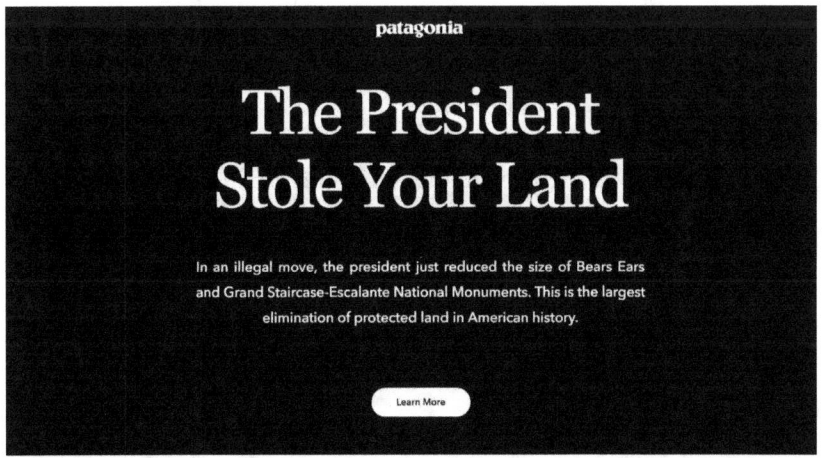

Patagonia wasn't being threatening or pessimistic. They were being real and sparking anger. (Remember, Hope has two daughters and one of them is Anger.)

If your positive message isn't working, how can you invoke anger?

In *Erosion: Essays of Undoing*, Terry Tempest Williams painted a picture of our national parks in 2055 if we continue treating the earth as we are now. If we do nothing.[47]

Her essay entitled *The Park of the Future* takes visitors to Canyonlands National Park. Access to the park is limited to two "enclosed viewing stations...that are cooled by solar power." The roads, now abandoned, are "historical scars reminiscent of a time when the world was fueled by gasoline and people drove cars without thinking."

Virtual goggles are provided at the lookout stations where visitors can look out at the now barren landscape and see what it looked like decades ago when there was sage, other greenery, trees, wildlife, and water in the river.

This essay has haunted me ever since I read it. I think how right Jane Goodall was about getting to the heart with story. You won't know it, but people will go on thinking.

Terry Tempest Williams brought the issue of climate change to life by showing us what is at stake. The problem of climate change is vast and daunting. Most of us care about it and do what we can by drinking water from our Hydro Flask water bottles and shopping with reusable bags. All while knowing it's not enough.

In choosing one park and scenario to represent a global issue, Williams changed my thinking. It holds real estate in my memory, which is a huge feat since I seem unable to remember much without writing it down. But I can't shake this story from my mind.

Change-makers get to the heart with a story and make us angry. We'll go on thinking. And eventually, we'll take action.

Positivity isn't always the answer—especially if it leads to false hope. If you are working on something that feels bigger than the individual; something that is daunting and even abstract, have you shown your audience what is at stake if nothing changes? You don't have to be alarmist or threatening, but clearly illustrate what it would look like if you didn't exist.

Show people a future that doesn't include you and them together.

The solutions should be within their capacity. If it feels hopeless, they turn away.

Give them impact, make them think, make you hard to shake from their mind. Then, they'll take action.

People need to know enough to understand what is at stake. We look away when faced with guilt or fear and feel helpless. We act on anger and hope when we know our actions can make a difference. A small contribution should be able to make a difference.

> ## Story prompts
>
> Ask what's at stake if they don't act.
>
> Where did this happen elsewhere? How was it solved? Or what happened when it wasn't?
>
> What accessible solutions are there? What easy steps can we take? What solutions are within reach?
>
> What's the bold, but positive, version of our negative story?

## Should we risk taking a stand on an issue?

Unlike Patagonia, you may not be in a position to make people angry. Perhaps you can't risk turning people away with your personal views. You worry about standing for something.

I had similar concerns as I drove to the airport early on the morning of June 24th, 2023. NPR announced that Roe v. Wade had been overturned. It wasn't a surprise, but it was a shock.

Tears streamed down my face. To think that people I didn't know could control my choices about my body made me feel violated. But I mostly felt (and still feel) fear and dread for so many women in the United States.

I wondered whether I should write about it in my biweekly newsletter, *The Power of Stories*. Would it be appropriate to talk about something I care about personally in a professional environment? Or should I keep my opinions to my personal interactions? I decided to talk about it because whether or not my readers share my viewpoint on reproductive rights, I knew I could tie it in with my work because it allowed me to make a point about leaders who take a stand.

For some, deciding whether or not to speak out is a difficult choice. There's no doubt you take a risk in standing up for something. Yet, if you are leading an organization, large or small, national or community, what does it say if you say nothing?

When you do, people will love you or hate you. When you don't, they'll be ambivalent.

When the Roe v. Wade overturn hit the news, I was working with an international company headed by a female CEO. She decided to delay a significant announcement scheduled for that day because she knew employees would be reeling from the news. She also quietly acknowledged that others might be celebrating it.

Reporting on a study conducted in early 2020, Harvard Business Review found that political advocacy, especially among millennials, is considered a natural extension to every business and a way for organizations to connect and build loyalty.[48] However, while people found it natural in cases of liberal advocacy, conservative views tended to garner a more negative reaction. More significantly, it found that women tend to react negatively regardless of their viewpoint.

## Story type: Provocative with purpose

When you reflect on your situation, there are many factors to consider, including the data cited from that study. More importantly, it reinforces the need for clear values at the outset. When you are clear about what you stand for, your board, your shareholders, and your people will be aligned.

If we look to Patagonia as a role model as they advocate for the environment, we can see how it makes sense for them. The story about President Trump stealing land is one of many examples. And each time they do so, they assuredly risk losing customers. But Patagonia doesn't care, because many *more* people decided this company is where they want to spend their money. (In 2023, the company's estimated revenue was $23.5 billion.)

They don't have to worry about losing shareholders and

employees because those who would be upset are long gone or never hopped on board to begin with. Instead, they have loyal fans who don't care how much it costs to buy a pair of running shorts because they love the brand and what it stands for.

As I write this, Taylor Swift is possibly the most popular person on the planet. She also has more than her fair share of haters.

When you stand for something, you create a community of people who love you so much that money is not part of the conversation. It's up to you to decide what matters—ambivalence or stronger bonds accompanied by anger from some.

I thought carefully about voicing my upset about the Supreme Court decision on Roe v. Wade. Do I care that someone is offended by my message and never works with me? No. If you disagree with me enough that it influences your decision, we shouldn't work together, as we likely hold different values.

When my client delayed that important internal announcement scheduled to go out the following day (June 24th), she instead shared a message of empathy on what they knew was a difficult day for many. Her staff appreciated the message and felt bonded to her.

At a minimum, people want to feel seen and heard, and a message that shows you care and are affected can go a long way.

Taking a stand is a risk each of us must weigh carefully. Being provocative will get you noticed, and it's important to be more than provocative. Being provocative with a *purpose* will do far more for you.

When we stand up for something, we attract the right people. People who uniquely *love* us, not just *like* us.

Being provocative with a purpose means you stand for something. It means you become a change artist in a sea of same. In an interview with Fast Company about his book *Unthink,* Erik Wahl lists the elements needed from an individual, professional development standpoint.[49,50] He suggests that we should step outside our bubble, live outside our comfort zone, ask for forgiveness rather than permission, and start small.

Doing so creates:

- Loyal fans: You're giving people a reason to love (and hate) you.
- Longevity: Your customers will return and spread the word about you.
- Resiliency: Brands have their ups and downs. Those who have built a community of loyal fans and a bank of goodwill have an easier time bouncing back from the downs.
- It can feel threatening to question the status quo, yet when we take a stand, we bring our loyal fans along.

### Story prompts

What is happening in the world right now that you care about?

What are your values and where are they being challenged?

How can you use your platform for positive change, ensuring it's aligned with the work you do?

# How can I make my stories inspirational?

I'm not a mom, but I know the secret to getting your kids to eat their broccoli: Cover it with melted cheese. Everything tastes delicious with cheese! How can we melt cheese on your story? I have an idea.

In 2014, Budweiser's Super Bowl commercial with the Clydesdales featured a puppy that was up for adoption at a neighboring farm. It kept escaping from the farm to visit one of the horses with whom it struck up a connection. The owner kept returning the puppy, but it kept going back until everyone realized the puppy and the horse needed to be together. The music crescendoed when the puppy and horse ran across the field together. It brings tears to my eyes every time I see it, but talk about cheesy! It's a sappy love story between a puppy and a horse in a contrived attempt to sell me bad beer. When the music crescendos, we have a formulaic tearjerker.

Budweiser is trying to melt cheddar cheese on my broccoli to get me to eat it. And I won't have it. I might cry, but I'm not buying Budweiser. Emotion isn't everything and I'm not falling for your tricks, Budweiser!

I want to offer a different idea of a story crescendo that is not cheesy. Rather, it's a great way to level up your stories and connect to a grander purpose.

Remember, people crave a connection to purpose. An important element of a riveting story is to elevate the story to connect to purpose.

## Story model: The question every story needs to answer

"So what?" That's the most important question you can ask before finalizing any story. What is this really about, and why should the audience care? You cannot be riveting without clear answers—in your mind and in the story.

An education alliance client funded a grant to bring a fiddle camp to an elementary school. On the surface, that sounds pretty unimportant compared with all the other pressing matters in the world today. Limiting the story to learning how to play the fiddle would likely be pretty boring.

We asked: "So what?" Well, it changed the culture in the school because everyone was so excited about a break in the academic curriculum.

"So what?" we asked again. Then we learned about a shy and reserved girl who got dressed up for her recital and gave an incredible performance despite her nerves. We had a beautiful photo of her in her dress on the stage. The true story, we realized, was about building self-confidence in youth. It was about pushing their boundaries and helping them step out of their comfort zones.

By asking "So what?" multiple times, you level up the abstraction and tie it into a theme that really matters and connects with purpose. Your story has many facets, but to make it riveting, you need to bring out the very thing that gets your audience excited.

> **Story prompts**
>
> So what? (If the ending of your story happens/is true, what can then happen?)
>
> Why does this matter to our audience?
>
> What is this story really about?

## Riveting is the story of the collective

When you get real, you ground your messages in evidence. Being relatable means to meet your audience where they are. Connecting to purpose and vision is riveting.

Riveting conversations are rooted in shared purpose. They are balanced between the teller and receiver (that's relatable), and they are connected to shared values. They make each of you better for having had the conversation. Rather than complaining and gossiping, they are driven by a desire to better each other or the world. They empower you to stand out and stand up for what you believe in rather than how you think you should show up.

Being riveted to something means it's fixed, fastened. Riveting stories fully engross your audience so they don't notice what's happening around them. These are the kind of stories that hold space in someone's heart and mind until they do something about it.

# PART IV

# THE COLLECTIVE IMPACT

# 12

# INFLUENCE IS EVERYTHING

When I returned from my summer exchange in France, I had to break the news to my mom about her favorite blouse. It was before the internet and texting, so we hadn't been in touch. That meant she was blissfully ignorant until I came home.

There were several ways I could have approached delivering this difficult message. I could have ignored it and hoped that she'd forgotten about the blouse. I could have pointed a finger at someone or something else. But, while I didn't know I'd write about it in a book someday, I decided the most ethical approach was to be real and relatable. I added some riveting for good measure.

In other words, I simply told the truth. And I did it while she was still so excited to have me home (the riveting part) that her delight overshadowed the disappointment. Remember, she didn't want to lend me the blouse.

When we get the connection right, we shift people from thinking rationally to thinking emotionally. I'm not saying we all can get away with burned blouses, but we do, with a storytelling habit over time, establish trust, relevance and hope. It doesn't happen overnight.

Jen Castle and Blake Spalding didn't raise $400k for their HBG restaurant because they were suddenly transparent.

Taylor Swift didn't spike the voter registration count because she sent a single tweet.

Patagonia founder Yvon Chouinard didn't even want to start a business. He just wanted better quality climbing gear.

It took a whole lot of relationship-building on a foundation of storytelling for these highly influential leaders to become change-makers.

# Trust

Trust is hard to earn, very easy to lose, and even harder to regain.

Many of us think we have earned it. But have we? A 2017 Vanguard whitepaper identifies the need for three types of trust: functional, emotional, and ethical.[51] Clients in the financial services space were more likely to trust their advisors when all three were met. However, the three are not evenly weighted. Some have a greater impact on trust than others.

Functional trust accounts for 17% of total trust. Your credentials, skills, day-to-day operations, and proactive communications contribute to functional trust.

Ethical trust accounts for 30% of total trust and means there is no conflict of interest, reasonable compensation and fees, and you are acting in the client's best interest.

Emotional trust accounts for 53% of total trust. These are

intangible aspects of the relationship. In financial management, it means they think the advisor is their advocate and makes them feel their portfolio is important. From a broader perspective, it means you are the best or only person to help them.

You can see where functional trust makes you think you have earned the trust of your audience, but emotional trust is what retains and expands your efforts. Emotional trust is the most significant, yet it's the one we consider least in everyday interactions.

I worked with a graphic designer for a few years because he got the job done, and I could count on him (functional trust). But he could be difficult to work with, and I didn't enjoy the overall experience. I never felt like we were partners in projects. I didn't even like riding in the car with him to projects. While we don't have to be friends with the people we work with, this person had not earned my emotional trust. Because of that, I was continually on the lookout for someone better. He wasn't the only one who could help me.

Emotional trust is built over time through your actions and the stories of your actions.

## Relevance

When you are real and relatable, you become relevant.

People know who you are, understand what you do, and what you stand for. When they have stuck with you and paid attention to you long enough to have all that, they know they want to be connected to you because you have shared values, objectives, or outcomes.

Alignment cuts through the noise. People can pick you out in a crowd, just as I did when I came into the finish line chute of a trail running race, exhausted and depleted. As I ran the final yards, I searched for my husband in the chaos of the cheering throng. I heard a quiet "Honey". He didn't yell or wave his arms. He didn't have to compete for my attention because I knew that voice. I turned my head to see his camera poised. I waved and finished my race. He achieved his objective—me smiling for the camera.

Relevance is the antidote to becoming obsolete. It is built over time through who you are and the stories of who you are.

# Hope

Hope is the parent of Anger and Courage. It keeps people on track. Why bother doing anything if there is nothing to hope for? The future is better with you around. You have established this by offering a clear picture of reality, creating understanding around a problem and a solution, and shifting perceptions to untangle misinformation. You have shown what is possible.

People act on anger (the reality and the problem) and hope (what is possible).

There could be a million other people doing what you do, but no one shares the unique combination of stories that make up who you are, what you've done and what you can do.

Your stories help you stand out instead of fit in.

# 13

# BUILD A STORY LIBRARY

Storytelling is powerful because it is a figurative lever. [52] You are busy, and your budgets are tight. Starting a storytelling effort feels risky and unproductive, because it takes a lot of time and it's new to you. Yet the opposite is true. In the end, stories will save you time and increase your return. Here's a client example to show you how.

I've had the awesome privilege of working with an education foundation for the past couple of years. Recently, they told me that their year-end fundraising campaign was off the charts. Better than ever.

Since the foundation began a regular cadence of storytelling, they have increased their fundraising by 6% ($47,000) in the first year, then another 16% in the second year for a total increase of $91,000. All done with a team of three.

How did they do it? Together, we focused on gathering one story per month. Those stories came from clients and leaders in the school district or community. We spoke to teacher grantees and students, business leaders, and state senators. We talked to donors, the founders, and the parents of students.

Each story might start as a blog post or a video, which was then shared on social channels.

But (and here's where the leverage comes in) all this effort was amplified to create a greater output. They'd done the work, and now it reaped the rewards.

Over time, my client developed a database of stories from which to draw. They were brimming with content rather than scrambling for something helpful to say.

They asked me to craft a letter from the executive director to accompany a year-end distribution. We wanted the letter to show donors the impact of their generosity and how the organization quickly adapted to the COVID-19 pandemic.

I dipped into the organization's story library for three grantee stories. When I sat down to write the cover letter, I identified themes that tied in with the objective. Those real student examples brought each theme to life in simple sentences.

Instead of speaking in generic terms, I cited an at-risk student who came alive talking about bee colonies. I described how a fifth-grader living under the poverty level came out of her shell when she dressed up and performed in her fiddle recital, and how an aspiring design student put his creative juices to work—all because of the organization and their donors.

Each story was *real* and *relatable*.

We then elevated the message to show that the organization's work is really about exposing students to new experiences that build self-confidence. There was a big crescendo finale, trust me.

It was *riveting*.

I sent the draft off to the executive director for approval, and she wrote back that it brought tears to her eyes. That year, their giving increased by 16% on the previous year.

The letter took me less than an hour to write, but the hard work of story gathering had already been done.

It's like the legendary story of Picasso, who was reportedly doodling on a napkin at a café when an admirer asked to buy the drawing. He agreed to sell it for a million francs. When the potential buyer exclaimed, "But it only took you a few minutes to draw that!" he replied, "Yes, but it took a lifetime to be able to create it." That's leverage.

Storytelling can be leveraged across multiple uses. Ultimately, it saves you time (even though it takes a great deal of time to do) and provides a greater return on your investment. You get rich content you can use in everything you do. Input from these stories gives you a deeper understanding of what you should be talking about, which saves time when you're staring at a blank screen, wondering what to include in that next email or report.

Stories work. It's all the same whether you are connecting to employees, customers, or donors.

Develop a bank of stories that you can use over time. You'll get better at it and refine the stories based on the feedback and reactions. You will start seeing stories everywhere, and you'll get into the habit of using them to connect to remain relevant and riveting.

In the end, you cannot afford not to become a storytelling leader.

# The ripple effect

As I'm writing this, I have just met with the education client after our quarterly newsletter had gone out. A journalist with the local paper wanted to cover the story within that newsletter and asked for an interview. She ended up writing two articles to show the impact this organization is having.

One story led to another, which led to another.

Who will see that story? Who will tell someone about it, and who will do something about it? Story is a powerful lever to get to hearts.

In James Clear's bestselling book *Atomic Habits*, he encourages readers to look at change through small steps, not massive leaps. Tiny habits have ripple effects and contribute to a greater collective impact.[53]

Think of your storytelling in the same way. You really can make change happen one story at a time.

The journey to get to know you can be long, winding, and unpredictable. A library of stories helps move people by answering their questions at any given time.

Real: anchor your stories in reality.

- Bio: Personal story, not history.
- Micro story: The headline.
- About Us: Organization's story, not history.
- Metaphor: Compare your message to something they know.

- The Myth buster: Overcome objections and misunderstandings and shift perception.
- The Elephant: Address the tough topics proactively.

Relatable: people act on things they understand.

- Your "Why:" Getting to know you.
- Care: When you care, they care.
- Problem, not solution: Sometimes they don't know the solution to the problem and only recognize the problem.
- Analogy: Reduce the psychological distance of the story by bringing it into their frame of reference.
- Visualize/Imagine if: Paint a vivid picture.

Riveting: shows people what is possible.

- Brand You: Bring your essence into everything you do.
- Referable: Get others to tell your story.
- Success stories: How you've helped others.
- Progress: Focus on the gain, not the gap.
- Provocative with purpose: Say what you stand for and challenge the status quo.

# 14

# THE LASTING POWER OF STORY

## The stories we tell ourselves

We get people to care through stories that are real, relatable, and riveting. But there is something more at play here: a bigger story.

Stories are the foundation of personal identity. What your parents and your teachers told you had a profound effect on shaping who you are today. Yet your stories go further than that.

Imagine this: It's the heat of summer. Too hot to think. You feel irritable, even a little foggy. The sun beats down, and you long for some shade and a cool breeze.

You head to the lake in the heat of the day for a plunge. You walk in up to your knees. Around you, kids are splashing and screaming, and babies are crying. Wave runners are buzzing, and you hear the thumping bass from the wakeboard boats out on the horizon. Waves push against you and crash noisily against the shore.

You raise your arms overhead and plunge into the water, arcing below the surface where everything peels away—the noise, the dirt, and sweat on your skin and the chaos. It is silent and cool, and you take a few extra strokes before coming up for air.

You break free of the surface and feel the sun on your face, but the noise and chaos are no longer as prominent. They don't affect you as they did seconds ago.

Now you can get back to work. The density of the heat weighing on you is gone.

In transcendental meditation (TM), the metaphor of the noise in the brain as an ocean is powerful.[54] The ocean is choppy and wavy on the surface; these are the stories we get mired in. They drag us down when we feel disappointed by a co-worker or an email that came through with just that tone. The surface is the monkey mind. Oh, the imagination that roams our monkey minds!

Deep in the sea below is a beautiful landscape with coral, stunning fish, and, best of all, pure silence.

The first time I went scuba diving, I jumped off the boat in four-foot swells. My mask pushed off my face, and the tank weighed a ton on my back. I could barely tread water, and I started to panic. I stopped to put my mask on, and, with oxygen flowing effortlessly, I sank below the surface. As instructed, I swam to the bow of the boat and took the line to sink 25 feet to the sea floor, where complete calm was restored.

The idea with transcendental meditation is that the more you access that deep quiet, the more you bring it to the surface of your everyday life.

The stories we tell ourselves on the surface change when we dive down to find undiscovered quiet and beauty.

Even more beautiful is that we can edit the stories we tell ourselves. This will be an important aspect of your storytelling journey—and it is the topic of my next book, *Rewriting Us*.

When we take control of our narrative, we can do powerful things together.

## Bridging divides

In November 2023, shortly after Hamas attacked Israel, taking hostages and killing hundreds, an American woman was at her son's soccer game. She heard a father from the opposing team speaking loudly in the bleachers, saying that Israel deserved the attack. The woman confronted him, irate, and the exchange escalated quickly to a shouting match.

In utter frustration, she pulled out her phone to show the man a photo of an 18-year-old family friend who was taken hostage. She pointed to both their 18-year-old sons on the field, safely playing as if nothing was happening in the Middle East. The conversation shifted as the man of Lebanese descent explained his view. Eventually, in tears, they hugged and parted ways.[55]

Even in the midst of deep divide, there is commonality. Stories can find that common ground. That is why Katherine Hayhoe, the lead scientist for The Nature Conservancy, wrote an entire book on the matter. In *Saving Us,* she describes the best way to talk about something so divisive: climate change.[56] Start with something in common, she says. Facts and data won't shift minds. Stories will. Connect to why climate change matters to you personally. If Hayhoe is speaking to a group of hunters, she references how their hunting grounds and prey will be impacted instead of how the earth is doomed and how, if we cared about the next generation, we'd do something about it.

Wicked problems such as climate change are social and economic problems. They are so complex that they are difficult to articulate and involve so many interdependent factors that they seem impossible to solve. Individuals can feel helpless in the face of wicked problems. When we connect the problem to their everyday lives and suggest small steps that can make a difference, we can bring people together regardless of their political ideology. One story at a time.

## Shaping worldviews

"There are probably two aspects of culture that stand out as being uniquely human. One is religion and the other is story-telling. There is no other species, whether ape or crow, that do either of these. They are entirely and genuinely unique to humans." So wrote Robin Dunbar in his book *Human Evolution*.[57]

Stories shape our view of the world from a very young age.

In *Braiding Sweetgrass,* Robin Wall Kimmerer shares the origin story of the First Nation peoples.[58] Sky Woman fell through a hole in the sky, and as she floated down to the sea, the animals below saw her impending doom. The geese put their wings together to hold her up while they sorted out how to support her. The turtle, floating in the sea, offered its dome to rest upon while the sea creatures searched for dirt she could settle on. Several creatures dove down to the sea floor to bring up some earth but were unsuccessful. Finally, the muskrat found mud at the bottom of the sea and gave its life to bring it back up. The remaining creatures spread the mud on the turtle while Sky Woman sang in thanksgiving, and the dirt expanded to create earth. She planted the seeds and plants she carried with her, and she and the animals benefitted.

It's a story of gratitude and reciprocity. The creatures helped Sky Woman; in doing so, she reciprocated with the plants, seeds, and skills that helped the animals thrive.

Imagine being told this story instead of the creation story in the Bible, where the serpent tempts Adam and Eve to eat forbidden fruit. They are subsequently banished from the garden, where they live out the rest of their days in toil and suffering.

A resource-based economy grew from the story of Adam and Eve, one in which supply and demand was a fundamental principle. We were taught that creating scarcity is good because it increases the price. Capitalism is good because if you work hard, you become rich. The winner takes all.

The story of Sky Woman is the seed for a very different set of beliefs grounded in indigenous culture where plants and animals are seen as gifts of the earth, and we must demonstrate reciprocity.

Kimmerer writes, "In Potowatomi, we speak of the land as emingoyak; that which has been given to us. In English, we speak of the land as 'natural resources' or ecosystem services."

Imagine as a child hearing the story of Sky Woman instead of Cinderella and Snow White, in which young girls are taught to be good and beautiful and wait for the prince to sweep them off their feet so they can live happily ever after.

The stories we are told at a young age unconsciously shape our worldview. What stories did you accept that have shaped how you see the world?

My wonderful grandfather used to say that talking about money is vulgar. I didn't even know what the word meant, but it sounded ugly, so I knew it was not right to talk about money. Grampa had the best intentions, but that saying created a negative story around money that impacted me for decades before I recognized it. Awareness was the first step. I have since worked through a new story that money is a good thing, not a bad thing. There is no shame in charging for my work or talking about it directly in meetings. When I can make a good living, I can help others thrive.

Thankfully, many of our unhelpful stories are changing. In 2023, *Barbie* became one of the highest-grossing movies of all time and the only female-dominated movie in that category. We are increasingly seeing stories that empower young women, and there's a growing feminist genre of fairy tales. There is no denying that stories shape and contribute to cultural worldviews.

People are ready for new stories. We are ready to break out of the status quo and look beyond gender, market economies, and natural resources. We are ready to embrace the gifts of the earth. To see things in new ways, to be emboldened.

If a story can do this much, I wonder what your story is capable of.

# 15

# WHAT'S NEXT?

You're doing good work. People don't know about it, don't get it, or aren't doing what you need them to do to give this work traction. Now you know that you need stories that are real, relatable, and riveting.

Imagine a world where you attract an audience of individuals who care about what you do. People seek you out, and you field requests and pick and choose what you want. The perfect candidates come to work with you. Your team is productive. Investors invest in you. Donors are abundant and help you make the change you were put in this world to do.

When we lead with story, everything gets better: our team and stakeholder engagement, revenue, and communities.

Leaders who want to make ideas happen don't have the luxury of working in isolation and silence. We have to get others on board with those ideas. We need relationships built on trust and understanding. Often considered a soft skill, storytelling is essential for any modern-day leader.

Your stories don't need to be epic dramas. They are handholds that start a conversation and give the receiver something to latch onto to discover and respond. People crave connection and purpose. Stories? They aren't really about stories. They are about connection. When you make connections, you increase your influence.

I invite you to put your stories out into the world. See what happens. I think you'll be pleasantly surprised. Adjust as needed. And if I can help, I'm here for you.

# WHO IS LISA?

I know that telling your own story is the hardest. How do you condense a lifetime of experiences into a few paragraphs? Yet, as a storytelling advocate and considering everything I've covered in this book, I must practice what I preach!

Here, then, is my story (not my history), to answer your essential question: Why should I listen to what Lisa has to say?

I am a storytelling strategist, speaker, author, and mentor working with established and emerging leaders. Together, we uncover their stories so they can build thriving teams, practices, and communities.

It wasn't always this way. I graduated college without a plan, so I followed the one thing I loved: skiing. I launched my hospitality career in Aspen, Colorado, which is a fancy way of saying I waited tables to support my skiing habit. One thing led to another, which led to a job with the Four Seasons Hotel in Seattle. Eventually, I put my communications degree to work in urban development and revitalization.

One sunny winter morning, my employer announced they had purchased a ski resort in Idaho, and that's when skiing and communications converged. What started as no plan looked like a grand plan in hindsight. I became a marketing director at a ski resort.

I've always seen how stories bring people together to solve big problems and make change happen, so in 2004 I left my dream job to do more of that. Since then, I have worked with entrepreneurs, leaders in technology, manufacturing, and global nonprofits to communicate more meaningfully with stories to shift team dynamics and bring communities together.

My coaching and training programs have transformed the way emerging and established leaders communicate. They have used story to fund education through a permanent tax levy, to secure millions in funding for conservation, and to earn the trust of thousands of employees in a global outdoor education company.

My first book, *From So What? To So Funded: How nonprofits use story to create impact and change the world* is available in your favorite online store.

When not in the office, you can guess where I'll be: skiing, trail running, or mountain biking with my husband and dogs. That's where I do my best creative thinking.

Uncovering your own story is best done with an outside perspective.

Every good story has a guide and I can be yours. I'd love to speak at your next off-site, host a retreat for your team, or work with you one-to-one so you can develop a storytelling habit that leads to growth.

You can connect with me on LinkedIn (https://www.linkedin.com/in/lisagerber/) or through my website, www.lisabgerber.com.

I look forward to continuing our conversation.

# REFERENCES

1. Goodall, J., Abrams, D.C. & Hudson, G. (2021). *The Book of Hope: A survival guide for an endangered planet.* Celadon Books.
2. Hasson, U. (2016). *This is your brain on communication.* [online] Available at: www.ted.com.https://www.ted.com/talks/uri_hasson_this_is_your_brain_on_communication?language=en
3. George Lakoff, G. (2024). George Lakoff. [online] Available at: https://george-lakoff.com [Accessed March 2024].
4. Lieberman, M.D. (2013). *Social: Why our brains are wired to connect.* New York, New York: Crown Publishers.
5. De Smet, A., Dowling, B., Mugayar-Baldocchi, M. & Schaninger, B. (2021). *How companies can turn the Great Resignation into the Great Attraction | McKinsey.* [online] www.mckinsey.com. Available at: https://www.mckinsey.com/capabilities/people-and-organizational-performance/our-insights/great-attrition-or-great-attraction-the-choice-is-yours [Accessed March 2024].
6. Harter, J. (2022). *Employee Engagement vs. Employee Satisfaction and Organizational Culture* [online] Gallup. Available at: https://www.gallup.com/workplace/236366/right-culture-not-employee-satisfaction.aspx
7. Consultancy.eu. (2020, October 19). The need for close client relationships in professional services. [online] Consultancy.eu. Available at: https://www.consultancy.eu/news/5090/the-need-for-close-client-relationships-in-professional-services [Accessed May 2024].

8. Gratton, P. (2024). *Trust: A Financial Advisor's Most Important Asset.* [online] Investopedia. Available at: https://www.investopedia.com/financial-advisor/trust-advisors-most-important-asset/

9. NPOInfo. (2023, December 7). *Web Analytics for Nonprofits: A Mini Guide for the New Year.* [online] NPOInfo. Available at: https://npoinfo.com/category/data-statistics/ [Accessed May 2024].

10. Stone, M.K. & Barlow, Z. (2005). *Ecological literacy: educating our children for a sustainable world.* San Francisco: Sierra Club Books.

11. Brown, B. (2010). *The Gifts of Imperfection.* Center City, Minn.: Hazelden.

12. www.netflix.com (n.d.). Miss Americana. Netflix Official Site. [online] Available at: https://www.netflix.com/ph-en/title/81028336 [Accessed April 2024].

13. Gerber, L. (2017). How to Stop Effing Up Your Email Marketing and Make More Connections. [online] Lisa Gerber. Available at: https://bigleapcreative.com/email-marketing-please-stop-effing-it-up/ [Accessed 3 September 2024].

14. Greathouse, J. (2017). My Mistake Led To LogMeIn Eclipsing GoToMeeting. *Forbes.* [online] 13 Feb. Available at: https://www.forbes.com/sites/johngreathouse/2017/02/11/my-mistake-led-to-logmein-eclipsing-gotomeeting/?sh=280ea9e61f7d [Accessed February 2024].

15. Bond, S. (2021). *A Pandemic Winner: How Zoom Beat Tech Giants To Dominate Video Chat.* [online] NPR.org. Available at: https://www.npr.org/2021/03/19/978393310/a-pandemic-winner-how-zoom-beat-tech-giants-to-dominate-video-chat [Accessed May 2024].

16. We and Me. (n.d.). Chad Littlefield - Author, Speaker, and Mentor. [online] Available at: https://weand.me/chad-littlefield [Accessed February 2024].

17. Reid, T. J. (2019). *Daisy Jones and The Six: A Novel.* Random House.

18. Wikipedia. (2018). Steve Jobs. [online] Wikipedia. Available at: https://en.wikipedia.org/wiki/Steve_Jobs

19. Sullivan, B. (2023). *A Taylor Swift Instagram post helped drive a surge in voter registration.* [online] NPR. Available at: https://www.npr.org/2023/09/22/1201183160/taylor-swift-instagram-voter-registration

20. Covey, S.R. (2013). *The 7 Habits of Highly Effective People: Powerful lessons in personal change.* New York: Simon & Schuster.

21. AP (1996). Seattle Boy, 4, Enthroned as a Lama in Nepal. The New York Times. [online] 29 Jan. Available at: https://www.nytimes.com/1996/01/29/world/seattle-boy-4-enthroned-as-a-lama-in-nepal.html

22. Brooks, D. (2022, September 29). *Building Trust and Connection.* [online], Aspen Ideas to Go. Available at: https://www.aspeninstitute.org/podcasts/david-brooks-on-building-trust-and-connection [Accessed February 2024].

23. Berger, W. (2016). *A More Beautiful Question: The Power Of Inquiry To Spark Breakthrough Ideas.* New York: Bloomsbury.

24. Gerber, L. (2019). Bill Gamber: Actions Speak Louder Than Marketing. [online] Lisa Gerber, Gear Show Podcast. Available at: https://bigleapcreative.com/bill-gamber [Accessed February 2024].

25. Lakoff, G. & Johnson, M. (1980). *Metaphors we live by.* Chicago: University of Chicago Press.

26. Kimmerer, R.W. (2013). *Braiding Sweetgrass: Indigenous Wisdom, Scientific Knowledge and the Teachings of Plants.* Minneapolis, Minnesota: Milkweed Editions.

27. Schulz, K. (2018, September 24). *Why Two Chefs in Small-Town Utah Are Battling President Trump.* [online] The New Yorker. Available at: https://www.newyorker.com/magazine/2018/10/01/why-two-chefs-in-small-town-utah-decided-to-sue-president-trump [Accessed April 2024].

28. Gerber, L. (2023). *The Secret to Irresistibility.* [online] Lisa Gerber. Available at: https://bigleapcreative.com/the-secret-to-irresistibility [Accessed February 2024].

29. Bergin, T. & Kerry, F. (2010, June 2*). BP CEO apologizes for "thoughtless" oil spill comment.* [online] Reuters. Available at: https://www.reuters.com/article/business/environment/bp-ceo-apologizes-for-thoughtless-oil-spill-comment-idUSTRE6515NQ/#:~:text=The%20BP%20chief%20had%20remarked,lives%20in%20this%20tragic%20accident [Accessed May 2024].

30. Griner, D. (2017, September 22). *This Ski Resort Turned One-Star Reviews Into a Five-Star Ad Campaign.* [online] Adweek. Available at: https://www.adweek.com/creativity/this-ski-resort-turned-one-star-reviews-into-a-five-star-ad-campaign [Accessed April 2024].

31. Bowles, M., Burns, C. & Hixson, J. (2022). *How To Tell A Story.* New York: Crown.

32. Hunt, B., Sudeikis, J. & Kelly, J. (n.d.). *Ted Lasso.* [online] Wikipedia. Available at: https://en.wikipedia.org/wiki/Ted_Lasso [Accessed May 2024].

33. Shepardson, D. & Lampert, A. (2024, March 25). *Boeing CEO Dave Calhoun to step down in shakeup amid safety crisis.* [online] Reuters. Available at: https://www.reuters.com/business/

aerospace-defense/boeing-ceo-calhoun-step-down-2024-03-25 [Accessed May 2024].

34. Freeman, P. (2022). *How to tell a story: an ancient guide to the art of storytelling for writers and readers.* Princeton, New Jersey: Princeton University Press.

35. Goodall, J. & Berman, P. L. (1999). *Reason for hope: A Spiritual Journey* (P. L. Berman, Ed.). Grand Central Publishing.

36. Brooks, D. (2022, September 29). *Building Trust and Connection*, [online] Aspen Ideas to Go. Available at: https://www.aspeninstitute.org/podcasts/david-brooks-on-building-trust-and-connection/

37. Williams, T.T. (2019). *Erosion: essays of undoing.* New York: Sarah Crichton Books.

38. Operation Smile (2011). Home. [online] *Operation Smile.* Available at: https://www.operationsmile.org/

39. Jacobsen, S. (n.d.). *What I Want Everybody to Know About Afghanistan.* [online] Their Story is Our Story. Available at: https://tsosrefugees.org/stories/what-i-would-want-everybody-to-know-about-afghanistan [Accessed 20 February. 2024].

40. Gilbert, E. (2019). *City of Girls: A Novel.* Penguin Publishing Group.

41. ABC News. (n.d.). *Video Scramble for US Speed Skaters at Olympics to Get a Winning Suit.* [online] ABC News. Available at: https://abcnews.go.com/WNT/video/scramble-us-speed-skaters-olympics-winning-suit-22528594 [Accessed 20 February 2024].

42. Horovitz, B. (2014, February 21). *Under Armour founder says it's not the suit.* [online] CNBC. Available at: https://www.cnbc.com/2014/02/21/under-armour-founder-says-its-not-the-suit.html [Accessed February, 2024].

43. www.cbsnews.com. (n.d.). *U.S. speed skaters struggle: Are high-tech suits to blame?* [online] Available at: https://www.cbsnews.com/news/winter-olympics-2014-are-high-tech-suits-to-blame-for-as-us-speed-skaters-struggles/ [Accessed December 2021].

44. Langdon, T. (2023, December 13). *When to Use Positive vs. Negative Emotional Appeals.* image works. [online] Available at: https://www.imageworksdirect.com/blog/when-use-positive-vs-negative-emotional-appeals [Accessed May 2024].

45. Yousef, M., Dietrich, T. & Torrisi, G. (2021, June 22). Positive, Negative or Both? Assessing Emotional Appeals Effectiveness in Anti-Drink Driving Advertisements. [online] *Sage Journals*. Available at: https://journals.sagepub.com/doi/10.1177/15245004211025068 [Accessed May 2024].

46. Sullivan, D. & Hardy, D. B. (2023). *10x Is Easier Than 2x: How World-Class Entrepreneurs Achieve More by Doing Less.* Hay House.

47. Williams, T. T. (2019). *Erosion: Essays of undoing.* New York: Sarah Crichton Books.

48. Bailey, J. R. & Phillips, H. (2020, February 17). *How Do Consumers Feel When Companies Get Political?* [online] Harvard Business Review. Available at: https://hbr.org/2020/02/how-do-consumers-feel-when-companies-get-political [Accessed February 2024].

49. Walter, E. (2013, July 17). *Unlock Your Creative Genius: 4 Steps To Being Provocative With A Purpose.* [online] Fast Company. Available at: https://www.fastcompany.com/3014314/unlock-your-creative-genius-4-steps-to-being-provocative-w [Accessed March 2024].

50. Wahl, E. (2013). *Unthink: Rediscover Your Creative Genius.* Crown.

51. Madamba, A. & Utkus, S. P. (2017, November 9). *Trust and Financial Advice*. [online] Vanguard Research. Available at: https://static.vgcontent.info/crp/intl/gas/canada/documents/trust-and-advice-research.pdf [Accessed February 2024].

52. Fink, C. (2021). *The Leverage of Speaking.* [online] Available at: https://www.colfink.com/articles/the-leverage-of-speaking [Accessed February 2024].

53. Clear, J. (2018). *Atomic Habits: An easy and proven way to build good habits and break bad ones.* Penguin Random House.

54. Wikipedia (2020). *Transcendental Meditation.* [online]. Available at: https://en.wikipedia.org/wiki/Transcendental_Meditation

55. NPR (2023). A family has one goal: to get back their son who vanished when Hamas attacked Israel. [online] NPR. Available at: https://www.npr.org/2023/10/30/1209377191/family-has-1-goal-to-get-back-their-son-who-vanished-when-hamas-attacked-israel [Accessed May 2024].

56. Hayhoe, K. (2021). *Saving Us: A Climate Scientist's Case For Hope And Healing In A Divided World.* New York, USA: Simon & Schuster.

57. Dunbar, R.I.M. (2014). *Human Evolution.* London: Pelican.

58. Kimmerer, R.W. (2013). *Braiding Sweetgrass: Indigenous Wisdom, Scientific Knowledge and the Teachings of Plants.* Minneapolis, Minnesota: Milkweed Editions.